The Phenomenon of Pentecost

The Phenomenon
of Pentecost

Frank J. Ewart

The Phenomenon of Pentecost

by Frank J. Ewart

8855 Dunn Road, Hazelwood, MO 63042
www.pentecostalpublishing.com

Library of Congress Cataloging-in-Publication Data

Ewart, Frank J.
   The phenomenon of Pentecost / by Frank J. Ewart.
       p.   cm.
   ISBN 0-932581-91-9
   1. Pentecostalism.   I. Title.
BR1644.E92   1992
270.8'2—dc20

91-37191
CIP

Contents

Preface 7

Introduction. 9

1. The Pentecostal Experience 21

2. The Church after Pentecost 31

3. The Challenge of Pentecost 43

4. The Revival in Topeka, Kansas 51

5. The Azusa Street Revival 61

6. Azusa Street Continued 73

7. Finished Work of Calvary and
Jesus Name Baptism 85

8. Baptism in the Name of Jesus Christ. 95

9. The Power of the Name 107

10. How the Jesus Name Message Came
to Canada, by Frank Small 119

11. Revival in Canada, by L. C. Hall 123

12. The Great Winnipeg Revival 127

13. The Great Outpouring in China. 131

14. The Gospel Invades India. 143

15. Pentecostal Leaders Rebaptized 155

16. Excerpt from *Meat in Due Season*. 161

17. The Miraculous Resurrection of Joe French,
by J. H. Duke. 169

18. Early Pentecostal Leaders. 175

Preface

Pentecost is experimental, not theoretical. The Savior of the world promised this supernatural experience and commanded His followers to tarry in Jerusalem until they received it. Inside one generation the known world rocked under their supernatural power. Can the assumption be sustained that this identical experience is available today? That it can. That it is enjoyed by multitudes in every land and available to all is the contention of this book.

Pentecost is a religion that defies definition. You cannot weigh, ticket, or analyze it by the methods used with other religions. It simply refuses to be catalogued with any of them. It deftly weaves human life into an adventure both interesting and fascinating. It brings Jesus Christ out of the hurly-burly of theological speculation and makes Him unspeakably real and precious.

The best of the wine of this life has been reserved for the last days of my long ministry. By the time this book gets into its print clothes, I will have celebrated my seventieth birthday. Fifty years of this time have been spent in the ministry of the Lord. A year and a half ago the stern verdict of medical science, based on x-ray examinations, was that because of a malignant cancer in the stomach I could not live. They gave me up to die. It did not matter what I did or what I ate, I was doomed to die in a few weeks or months. But the Almighty Physician said, "This sickness is not unto death, but for the glory of God, in order that the Son of God may be glorified thereby" (John 11:4).

I was able to take this word at face value, and believing that God would spare my life so that I could write this book, I began to mend. The devastating pain of the cancer left, and the writing of this book became my "life preserver." So these last months of my life have brought the greatest demonstration of God's Word, to which my long ministry has been a devotion.

I have ambitions for posthumous fame, but these are within narrow limits: that the many thousands of children that I have begotten in the gospel and the many that have been given a helping hand, when they hear that my voice is hushed and my pen laid down will drop a tear and thank God that I have lived.

EDITOR'S NOTE: This revised edition (2000) preserves the full text of the original book (1947). The following changes have been made: (1) Reorganization of the chapters in chronological order. (2) Addition of explanatory notes, new chapter titles, and missing Scripture citations. (3) Editing of capitalization, punctuation, spelling, and diction to conform to current Word Aflame Press house rules. (4) Correction of a few minor errors.

Introduction

The writer of this book had a long journey from his conversion to the miraculous experience that is the capstone of all others in the flesh—the baptism with the Holy Ghost and fire, with the Bible sign of speaking in other tongues. A personal reminiscence would probably be in order at this point.

I was born in Bendigo, Victoria, Australia, in 1876. My father was Scotch and my mother of Irish descent. After I had graduated from school I entered into the varied life that the sawmills, lumber woods, and bush life affords. I loved every form of athletic work, and early in life I became a good cricketer and a proficient foot-runner. I cherished the ambition of entering that profession with its questionable involvements of gambling. However, at the very threshold of this career God apprehended me with a better vision—the vision of a new racing career for an imperishable prize.

I had a vision one day of Christ on the cross. His hair was all disheveled and blood bespattered, and His lovely face white with agony. I can never forget the expression in those large, luminous eyes as they looked down on me from the cross of shame. I thought I heard a voice saying, "I died for you!" Then the vision passed. But it changed my life. I had visited Golgotha; I had seen humanity hanging on a tree in Christ, its federal head.

The ambition for worldly fame and popularity vanished from my horizon, and I surrendered my heart to

Christ and dedicated my life to the new vision of service for Him.

I enlisted in a new race that day. I became temperate in all things. I had to lay aside every weight and the sin that doth so easily beset me and run with patience the race set before me. Oh, what a change! I was in dead earnest from the start of this new career. I would get everything out of Calvary that God put into it. I would appropriate Christ in His fullness. He said that He died for me. That was enough! I would cease looking at the bleachers for their applause. I would seek that honor that comes from God only.

My early ministry as a bush missionary in Victoria was attended by unusual success. All I had was my experience and an insatiable hunger for knowledge of the Word of God. I studied and prayed while other men slept. I would often go to sleep while at study and wake up with the smell of my hair singed in the candle on the table. When I got a revival going, they would send up a man from the Baptist church headquarters to take over and I would move on to other pioneer work. In 1903 my health broke, and the doctors told me that I had not enough blood in my body to live on. They advised a change of climate.

I had some relatives in Canada, the country we Australians called Our Sister of the Snow! So I set my face towards that New World. Many almost insurmountable obstacles beset me in this purpose, but I never wavered, and I would say to my people: Canada is the place for me! In June of that year, I sorrowfully bid good-bye to the old life, its allurements and endearments, and sailed across the South Pacific Ocean. I landed at Vancouver and at once took a train for Weyburn, a town in the province of Saskatchewan, near where my cousin lived on a farm.

I presented my credentials to the officials at the Baptist headquarters in Winnipeg and was given a church pastorate. I married a Christian girl of a family of Baptists. I was reordained and worked for a few years at two different pastorates. However, the old insatiable hunger for a real experience with the Word of God still possessed me. My wife and I would come home from the Sunday's services and would get down and weep and pray for the power of the Holy Ghost to be manifested in our ministry as it was in Finney's and Moody's ministries.

God is always on hand to satisfy the longing soul and fill it with His goodness. There came a letter from my brother-in-law inviting us to come out and rest at his farm near New Westminster, British Columbia. He told us of some religious prodigy that had invaded that territory. He said it had everything in the religious world backed clean off the map. He said the pastor and every bonafide member of the church claimed to have received the baptism with the Holy Ghost, with the sign of speaking in other tongues as the Spirit gave them utterance, exactly as the early saints and apostles of the Lord Jesus received it. He said that many claimed divine healing, and they also claimed that the gifts of the Spirit were still available, as these had never been withdrawn from the church of Christ.

My physical trouble became worse, and in a few weeks we received a furlough from the church and were on our way rejoicing. We attended a few of their meetings, but hearing of a large camp meeting at Portland, Oregon, [in 1908] we decided to go there and see the new thing at its best.

I can never forget the first day I spent on that campground. The place seemed to be hallowed with the presence of the Deity. A strange, unearthly feeling possessed me, and I walked around attending every meeting and talking to everyone I could about this wonderful experience. I perceived with my own eyes and ears miracles that were indisputable being performed by the power of faith in the Word of God. Drunken men brought in on the gospel wagon from the street meetings would be sobered up, saved, and filled with the Holy Spirit, speaking in tongues. I would select those who gave the most wonderful testimonies and accost them after the meetings with: "I heard your wonderful testimony. I can't bring myself to believe that God is doing such things for His people. Is it on the level? My life is in the balance; everything depends on my getting this thing and getting it straight." Then they would go over it again and graciously assure me that it was for me, as God was no respecter of persons.

Then the great miracle happened. I got an insatiable hunger for this experience and commenced tarrying. I prayed night and day for twenty-one days. At midnight, as the twenty-first day ended, I received a mighty infilling with the Holy Ghost. God left no room for doubt. I spoke in several known languages that I knew nothing about, and some of them were interpreted that night. I had asked the Lord to let all diseases go out of my body when the Holy Spirit came in. He took me at my word and answered my prayer. I had been wearing glasses for years, but my eyes were completely normal again, and the new blood pulsated through my veins like a mountain stream. I felt like the psalmist, "I have run through a troop; and . . . leaped over a wall" (Psalm 18:29).

I left that camp with my new life and Holy Ghost power and the confidence that I could conquer every opposing force. I was soon disillusioned. The Baptist church refused to allow me to minister. I was summoned before the head of the church board in Winnipeg, who pleaded with me to recant even enough to say that people could get the baptism of the Holy Spirit without speaking in other tongues. I felt that I could not compromise that point.

Then this dignitary started to deride my experience and me. "What is the use of this new tongue you speak?" I said that I didn't know and didn't care. Then with a touch of blasphemy, he said, "Let me hear you speak in tongues as the Spirit gives you utterance, and I'll tell you what I think of it." I felt pained at the heart, but instantly God took my tongue and spoke a language that he was familiar with. I noted that he turned exceedingly pale. He asked no more questions and courteously dismissed me. God's judgment fell on that great man and he shriveled with disease and died on an operating table in a short time after our interview.

The church turned us away, but God opened up the way for service in new fields of labor. Ever since that time I have been at the head of a Pentecostal church.

In the year 1911, I came to Los Angeles, and the following year I assumed the pastorate of Brother Durham's great church. This continued until a year after Durham died. When the worldwide camp meeting started in Los Angeles in April 1913, I was ready for God's new move.

That this Pentecostal movement has suffered almost as many harms from its exponents as it has from its opponents is a lamentable fact. The precious people of

God who received this heavenly experience seemed to forget that in giving us His Holy Spirit the Deity had made an infinite investment in us. He invested His Word in us, His honor, and His truth. He has so identified Himself with His people that because Saul of Tarsus had been persecuting the saints the Lord could say to him: "Saul, Saul, why persecutest thou me?" (Acts 9:4). Not realizing what an inseparable unit the church and the Lord became by the baptism with the Holy Spirit, the precious, guileless saints of God indulged in much independent and external word and action that belied this great fact and so brought reproach on His name.

When Dr. R. A. Torrey wrote his awful, vehement tract against the Latter Rain Movement,[1] he called it "The Tongues Movement." He concluded it was emphatically not of God on seven propositions. One of these was that the movement was productive of more immorality and looseness than any other religious unit in Christendom. I answered the irate doctor in *Meat in Due Season*.[2] I said that this movement was a twin brother of the church that the apostle Paul founded in Corinth. There were lots of immoral deeds committed by the saints then, but each one was dug up and brought to light that it might be judged. If the Holy Spirit was as deficient in His operation of convicting of sin as He seemed to be in the nominal churches, these things never would have been uncovered.

As long as the leaders under God kept humble in this movement they were honored of God, but when they indulged in vainglory and emphasized the spectacular, God ceased to commit Himself to them. (See John 2:23-25.)

The writer was personally acquainted with Aimee

Semple McPherson and preached with her before she was married the second time. She came back from China a brokenhearted woman, having left her first husband over there in the cemetery. She told us at that time that she had completely lost her faith, but after much contrition and prayer she got back to God. She had the gift of prophecy and interpretation and a real gift of discernment.

This is true of all God's great servants. In their God-given humility lay the basis of their power and influence. When one vanished, the other diminished and slowly died out. When I would interrogate the late, lamented George B. Studd regarding the secret of Moody's power, he would think for a while and then look at me and say, "Dwight L. Moody was a humble man." That was enough; there was no need to say anymore. That was Moody's biography.

When Alexander Dowie lost his humility he lost his power to heal the people, and God ceased to commit Himself to him. He died an ignominious death, but before he died he sat on the platform of the Christian Catholic Tabernacle for three months in the meetings but was not permitted to speak. The man who wielded the powers of omnipotence and whose fame was worldwide dwindled to a hissing and a byword among his own people.

The experience of the Lord coming in to live in our hearts and making our bodies His habitation makes people truly humble. We have this treasure in earthen vessels that the power may be seen to be of God and not of us. Paul said, "Not that we are sufficient of ourselves to think any thing as of ourselves; but our sufficiency is of God; who also hath made us able ministers of the new testament; not of the letter, but of the spirit: for the letter killeth, but the spirit giveth life" (II Corinthians 3:5-6). Paul's thorn in the flesh was given to him to save him from becoming inflated with the transcendent revelations given him. He said that he was a boxer who hit hard and straight at his own body and led it away into captivity, lest after he had preached to others, he might become a castaway, or be rejected. (See I Corinthians 9:27, *Weymouth*.)

All the great leaders under God in this Latter Rain Movement sat at the feet of the Master long enough to learn this great secret of power. The fact that we have retained the power for four decades in a remarkable measure is owing to the fact that there are still a preponderating minority who realize that "except the LORD build the house, they labour in vain that build it" (Psalm 127:1). The fact that we have lost the glory and grandeur of the Lord's presence in our meetings to such a lamentable degree is because we have come to rely on so many other things. But one great thing is needful, namely, the consciousness of the Holy Spirit's indwelling.

When I came into this great movement by the baptism of the Holy Spirit over thirty-eight years ago, I found a burning bush in the midst of the people. The bush is burning yet, but its radiant glory has noticeably diminished. It is only a faint spark compared to the blazing shekinah of Azusa Street Mission.

All the great men of God—great in ratio as they were humble—would simply guide the worship in the Spirit so that God could get the very highest glory out of each meeting. Back in the beginning we were not so zealous to guard the doctrinal status as we were to maintain the spiritual status. A former Pentecostal leader who had become pompous and been laid on the shelf came into a humble pastor's meeting. He sat down in the seat of the scornful, and after the meeting he accosted the pastor, who was evidently ready for him. "Who runs this meeting?" he asked pertinently. "The Lord God runs this meeting, brother," said the pastor. "Oh, yes, I know, but who has charge of the meeting?" "None other but the Holy Ghost, my brother," answered the pastor. The questioner became irritated. "Well, who is head of the meeting?" he asked. "Why, none other than the Lord Himself," was the answer.

The interrogator looked at the pastor, and asked, "And pray, what do you do?" "Oh, I just keep the place in order and instruct the saints to let the Lord have His way with them." This humble attitude was the very secret of power in these Pentecostal meetings in the beginning, and it is today. Point me out the men in this movement whom God delighteth to honor, from Brother W. J. Seymour to the great leaders of the present day, and I will show you men who realize that their greatest asset is a God-given humility. When they lose that, they are like Samson shorn of his locks.

When God baptized us with the Holy Spirit, He ignited a tiny spark within each of us, which commenced to burn up our innate selfishness, pomp, and vain glory. If we put this fuel on the fire without holding back, the work went on, shaping us into the image of the Son of God. If we do not let this sacrificial fire upon the altar of our hearts burn up our carnality, then we will end up where we began—mere carnal Christians. We have virtually defeated God's purpose in apprehending us. For everyone who has received the Holy Spirit baptism is predestined to be conformed to the image of His Son.

This Latter Rain Movement is truly the "religion of the burning heart"! We can all still say from experience, "Did not our hearts burn within us, while he talked with us by the way, and while he opened to us the scriptures?" (Luke 24:32).

We are nearing the end of the church age; the signs are all around us. Judgment has begun at the house of God. The saints are going through experiences such as they never did before. At the end of the church age, the Master comes to the great dead body called the Laodicean church. The omniscient physician shakes His locks, hoary with eternity, as He diagnoses the case. No chill! No fever! "Neither hot nor cold! And because thou art neither hot nor cold, I will spue thee out of my mouth." (See Revelation 3:16.) That means judgment!

My prayer is that we may be identified as the church of the Philadelphians, who will let the fires of brotherly love so burn in us and toward one another that it will be said as in the beginning: "Behold how these Christians love one another!" Amen.

ENDNOTES

[1]Like most early Pentecostals, Ewart called the Pentecostal revival that began at the turn of the century The Latter Rain Movement. The reader should not confuse this name with the movement that began about 1947, the year of Ewart's death.

[2]Ewart published and edited *Meat in Due Season*, a periodical in which he expressed his Pentecostal views and doctrines. This publication had a large circulation and was very influential in spreading the Oneness message across North America and to foreign nations.

CHAPTER ONE

The Pentecostal Experience

Pentecost was the most important day in the history of the human race. It gathered into itself the purpose and plan of God in the creation of man. The great memorial days of Christendom, such as the birth of Christ, the death of Christ, and the resurrection of Christ, emptied themselves in essence into the great Day of Pentecost. Christ was the Lamb of God slain from the foundation of the world, and He was slain in the purpose of God in order that the world might have a Pentecost.

All the great types emphasize this divine arrangement. The two outstanding ones are the smiting of the rock in the wilderness and the baking of the two loaves with leaven, as one of the feasts of the Lord. God deliberately allowed the people to get thirsty in a place where there was no natural relief for their thirst. The rock clearly typified Christ. They drank of a spiritual rock that went with them and that rock was Christ. The smiting of the rock by Moses was a type of Calvary, where the rock of ages was smitten in order to get the living water—the Holy Spirit—which was poured out in abundance on the Day of Pentecost.

In the record of the typical feasts of Jehovah as recorded in Leviticus 23, we find the very significant linking of the three feasts that set forth the plan of God culminating in Pentecost. The Feast of Passover, typifying Calvary, was followed by the Feast of First Fruits, a type of the resurrection of Christ. In this significant feast the sheaf of wheat representing the body of Christ in resurrection was cut while the crop was yet standing, and the high priest waved it before the Lord. At Pentecost we have the wheat crushed and kneaded and baked with leaven into two loaves of bread—no longer a union of separate growths loosely bound together, but a real indivisible union of particles making one homogeneous body. This is the deeper meaning of Pentecost: "For as the body is one, and hath many members, and all the members of that one body, being many, are one body: so also is Christ" (I Corinthians 12:12).

When Jesus was crucified on the cross of shame between two thieves, it caused the utter demoralization of the discipleship or brotherhood formed by our Lord and called the twelve apostles. They all forsook Him and fled. The extent of the utter chagrin and crushing disappointment of the apostles is almost inconceivable. Crucifixion was reserved for the most culpable criminal. No Roman citizen could die by crucifixion. It was the most shameful mode of capital punishment known. It was invented by the ferocious Carthagenians and later adopted by the Romans.

The Master's reiterated teaching that He would rise from the dead never penetrated their minds, made opaque by the national belief that the Messiah would suddenly appear as a mighty, irresistible potentate and restore the Davidic theocracy in Jerusalem. Even after Peter had received the effulgent flash of revelation and cried out: "Thou art the Christ, the Son of the living God," he quickly dropped into his former insensibility to the great truth and assured Jesus that they would fight rather than let Him be apprehended by the Romans: "Be it far from thee, Lord: this shall not be unto thee!" (Matthew 16:16, 22). When He miraculously fed the multitude in the wilderness, the disciples joined in the desire of the crowd that He assume the kingship. When He sent away the crowd and commanded them to cross the lake, they were disappointed and chagrined, almost to the point of breaking up the brotherhood. The two disciples in the Emmaus road expressed the utter hopelessness that His death had produced in the hearts and minds of His disciples: "We trusted that it had been he which should have redeemed Israel" (Luke 24:21).

The Jewish national feasts had proceeded in their usual order, unmolested by the tragedy of Golgotha. Even the Feast of First Fruits and the reappearance of their Lord failed to reestablish their loyalty to Him as their Messiah. The many infallible proofs of a literal and tangible resurrection only provided periodic tonics to their mental capacities. They had mapped out a royal pathway to a glorious throne in Jerusalem but were not prepared for the sudden arrest, the indignities of the judgment hall, and the cross of shame.

When they met Him by appointment on the Mount of Olives, they disclosed their undying hope for David's restored theocracy: "Lord, wilt thou at this time restore again the kingdom to Israel?" (Acts 1:6). His answer was in harmony with His repeated teachings that the time of the setting up of God's kingdom was a secret. However, the promise of the Father was reiterated: "Ye shall receive power, after that the Holy Ghost is come upon you: and ye shall be witnesses unto me both in Jerusalem, and in all Judaea, and in Samaria, and unto the uttermost parts of the earth" (Acts 1:8).

The descent of the Holy Spirit on the Day of Pentecost forever banished the disciples' misapprehension and doubt. The cowards of the crucifixion were transformed into the heroes of Pentecost. Their words and actions were no longer hesitant but manifested triumphant certainty. Even Peter, the man who basely denied Him, was completely transfigured. The experience of the Holy Spirit baptism had the effect of merging the disciples into one concrete organism. Before that event there had been no organic unity, either in consciousness or fact, among the followers of Jesus. This unique experience formed the basis of a solidarity which transcended all other concepts of unity known. It surpassed them as the members of a living organism transcend the separate members of an organization. This innate consciousness could no more be ignored than the unity of hand or foot with the mind. No wonder that Paul in referring to this accomplishment of the baptism with the Holy Spirit wrote, "For in fact, in one Spirit all of us—whether we are Jews or Gentiles, slaves or free men—were baptized to form but one body." (See I Corinthians 12:13.)

Fifty days were counted from the former feast day to the great feast of Pentecost, and the celebration was in the exact manner that had prevailed throughout succeeding centuries. Great crowds of people came from the surrounding countries to the city of David during this festal occasion. Every avenue of approach was choked with pilgrims. The Temple built by King Herod to eclipse all its architectural predecessors was the center of attraction. It was situated in the heart of the city and covered seventeen acres of land. Its spacious areas were packed with a great concourse of people from far and near.

The disciples of Jesus had obeyed His instructions by tarrying in a compartment of the Temple—probably in Solomon's porch—and they tarried for ten full days, until the great day struck. Early in the morning with the suddenness of a blast of wind, the place where they were assembled was filled with the presence and power of the Deity. Jesus, in describing this to Nicodemus, said, "The wind bloweth where it listeth, and thou hearest the sound thereof, but canst not tell whence it cometh, and whither it goeth: so is every one that is born of the Spirit" (John 3:8). Cloven tongues of fire appeared upon their heads and they were all filled with the Holy Spirit and began to speak in foreign languages as the Spirit gave them words to utter.

The noise of 120 people speaking in foreign languages simultaneously must have made a noise like the roar of Niagara. It brought the multitude rushing together to see this new thing. They were completely confounded by this ecstatic, miraculous utterance; everyone heard a message in his own native language. This was the greatest miracle of the ages. Back at Babel's tower God had come down and confounded their language, but at Pentecost God came down and the confusion of Babel gave way to the harmony with the Holy Spirit, and the racial gaps of the centuries were miraculously bridged.

Let us pause long enough to try to visualize this tremendous spectacle of 120 ignorant Galileans simultaneously speaking languages that they had never learned—"foreign languages" (Weymouth); "other kinds of tongues" (Rotherham); "other languages" (Emphatic Diaglott). They were overpowered, influenced beyond control by the Holy Spirit, and suddenly became proficient linguists. No wonder the spellbinding effect produced upon the congregation is described in such words as: "They were beside themselves with wonder." The leading spokesman in abusive derision said, "These men are full of new wine." (See Acts 1:12-13.) It must have been a scene of seeming confusion to the natural mind. But the apostle cried, "These are not drunken, as ye suppose, seeing it is but the third hour of the day, but this is that which was spoken by the prophet Joel" (Acts 2:15-16). It would seem bad enough to the religious leaders for the apostles to allow such a confusing thing to happen, but to take it as a fulfillment of the prophetic and sacred roll was outrageous and amounted to utter sacrilege. These same guardians of religious worship had cried out in indignant protest when the multitude burst forth in praises when the King rode into Jerusalem on an unbroken ass. Even the little children joined in that noisy adoration, and when the scribes complained, Jesus answered, "Yea; have you never read, Out of the mouth of babes and sucklings thou hast perfected praise?" (Matthew 21:16).

Seventeen nationalities were present, and they all

heard God's message in their own language. This is what amazed the multitude, and the record runs, "They were all amazed and marvelled, saying one to another, Behold, are not all these which speak Galileans? And how hear we every man in our own tongue, wherein we were born?" (Acts 1:7-8).

This experience brought the religion of Christianity out of the realm of the theoretical into the experimental, which made it different from every other religion on the face of the earth. The Holy Spirit had come. It was Christ on the inside—"Christ in you, the hope of glory" (Colossians 1:27)—making good in us what He did for us, making the cross's work experiential, so that we can say, "I am crucified with Christ: nevertheless I live . . . and the life which I now live in the flesh I live by the faith of the Son of God, who loved me and gave himself for me" (Galatians 2:20).

Pentecost brings the glorified Christ into His temple, our bodies. There He dries our tears, comforts our hearts when they bleed, solves our problems, fights our battles, and bears our burdens. Pentecost is the living, abiding, continuous demonstration of the whole evangel of Christ. There are many reasons that a new language should be the sign of the baptism with the Holy Spirit. But the chief reason is that He comes in to take possession of us as His temple. Our bodies become the temple of the Holy Ghost. He takes over the purchased possessions. He takes our tongues and operates them in a miraculous announcement of the fact that our bodies are no longer our own, that we have been purchased with a price, that we are to glorify Him in our bodies and our spirits, which are His. This sublime, unspeakable, momentary consciousness is the greatest asset of the real child of God. He makes the fact of our sonship real and steps out of the dead ashes of history to become the greatest reality of our lives.

On the Day of Pentecost the apostle Peter became God's mouthpiece, the official spokesman of the King of glory. His amazing earnestness and fluency created the reverent attention of his audience. He contemptuously swept aside the irreverent taunt that the disciples of Jesus were intoxicated: It was prohibited either to eat or drink at this feast until after the third hour of the day. Then he launched into his enraptured declamation. His theme was that Jesus is the Messiah. This was the most objectionable theme to the Jews, for they had summarily rejected Jesus' claim to be the Messiah and condemned Him to death by crucifixion on the charge of blasphemy. In the wisdom given him by the Holy Ghost, Peter removed every possible Jewish objection to his theme before he announced it. He proved by the utterances of David in the Book of Psalms that the Messiah was first to die, be buried, and be raised from among the dead before He could sit on the throne of Israel. That David, himself being a prophet, had prophesied Christ's resurrection: "Thou wilt not leave my soul in hell, neither wilt thou suffer thine Holy One to see corruption" (Acts 2:27). These startling declarations were used as a basis for the conclusion: "Therefore let all the house of Israel know assuredly, that God hath made that same Jesus, whom ye have crucified, both Lord and Christ!" (Acts 2:36).

Stung to the heart, they cried out, "Men and brethren, what shall we do?" Then Peter answered, "Repent and be baptized, every one of you in the name of Jesus Christ for the remission of sins, and ye shall receive the gift of the

Holy Ghost" (Acts 2:37-38). He continued his exhortation until three thousand were obedient to the new faith. These continued steadfastly in the apostles' doctrine and fellowship and the breaking of bread and prayers. And fear came upon every soul and many wonders and signs were done by the apostles.

Thus the first Christian church was launched with 3,120 charter members. Jesus called this institution "my church," saying, "upon this rock I will build my church; and the gates of hell shall not prevail [close] against it" (Matthew 16:18). Thus it would seem that in the secret counsels of the Deity, the launching of the greatest enterprise of human history was reserved for a special time. Judaism had utterly apostatized. The Temple rituals had become demoralized and the sacrificial system had degenerated into a commercial racket. The Master had called it a house of merchandise and a den of thieves. The displeasure of God was manifested in the cleansing of the Temple and the rending of the sacred veil that barred any intrusion into the Holy of Holies. The resurrection of Jesus and the restoration of the apostolic brotherhood carried conviction to the wicked hearts of the high priest and his cohorts, and prepared the way for the crushing climax of Pentecost.

The apostle Peter's sermon carried conviction to the hearts of the great multitude; repentance was granted to three thousand, and these obeyed the apostolic instructions and became the charter members of the first Christian church. Peter had been a moral and mental delinquent. Weak and unstable, he had denied the Master with bitter oaths. But the coward of Gethsemane became the hero of Pentecost. His words were like blazing syllables of fire. He stood forth as a shining, seraphic soul, vibrating with verbal inspiration—dramatic, trenchant, penetrating, and forceful. His sermon was a mingling of the terrors of the divine law and the tender solicitudes of divine grace. No wonder the great concourse of people were moved as a field of corn by a tornado, and multitudes were convinced, convicted, and converted.

The feast of Pentecost, after being shrouded in mystery and cloaked in obscurity throughout the centuries, was at last fulfilled. The two loaves, signifying the two divisions of the human race, Jew and Gentile, were kneaded and baked. This was the operation that had made of the twain one new man. The multiplied divisions of the human family with their Babel of languages could now become citizens of Zion, the city of the living God, and speak a pure language. Amazing, grand, glorious, divine!

CHAPTER TWO

The Church after Pentecost

The inspired church history in the Book of Acts is the only absolutely reliable history we have. Its records cover a period of over thirty years. A close, unbiased study of these records would seem to show conclusively that the phenomenon of Pentecost was practically repeated in essence in every subsequent revival. As it was a well-established fact that speaking with other tongues as the Holy Spirit gave utterance was the initial manifestation or sign of the reception of the Spirit baptism, the historian Luke did not think it necessary to record this fact in every case. However, the fact remains that in the revival at Caesarea, the picture is dramatically drawn of a section of Jewish Christians—"men of the circumcision" who accompanied the apostle Peter from Joppa—being unalterably opposed to the apostle's preaching the gospel to the Gentiles. They evidently argued with Peter all the way en route. However, when God interrupted Peter's sermon and baptized all who heard the word with the Holy Spirit exactly as the Jewish believers had received the Spirit, the record runs: "And they of the circumcision which believed were astonished, as many as came with Peter, because that on the Gentiles also was poured out the gift of the Holy Ghost. For they heard them speak with tongues, and magnify God" (Acts 10:45-46).

At Ephesus the same audible and visible manifestations occurred. At the great revival mentioned in Acts 4:4, where the number of believers was increased to five thousand, it is not recorded that they received the Holy Spirit with the sign of speaking with other tongues, but neither is it mentioned that they repented and were baptized in water. But no one would risk his honesty by denying that they did repent and were baptized in water.

At Samaria there was a great revival under the evangelist Phillip, and again Luke did not mention that those who received the Holy Spirit by the laying on of the apostles' hands after they became believers spoke with new tongues. However, we know they did by the fact that when Simon saw that through the laying on of the apostles' hands the Holy Ghost was given, he wanted to purchase the power to produce the same effects on people by the laying on of his hands. He must have observed an outward, audible, and visible manifestation to cause him to make the startling and blasphemous proposal he made to the apostle, and by which he nearly forfeited his life. The Greek words translated "when Simon saw" would be more accurately rendered "when Simon perceived." This made several accredited commentators observe that the manifestations at Samaria must have been substantially synonymous with those at Ephesus and at Pentecost, in which cases they spoke with new tongues.

The records of Paul's conversion do not say that he received the Holy Spirit and spoke with tongues, but we know assuredly from his own testimony and teachings that he did. It would not seem consistent with the Word of God in its entirety that God would give His saints unequal experiences. Things that are equal to the same thing are also equal to one another. If Acts 2:4 describes "the same thing" and the record runs that they were all filled with the Holy Spirit and began to speak in other tongues as the Spirit gave them utterance, then it follows that all who were filled with the Holy Spirit also spoke with other tongues.

This was the spiritual analogy of the "early rain," and the downpour lasted beyond the first century, dating from Pentecost. Towards the middle of the second century (A.D.), the historian notes a decided decline of apostolic power and glory. This decline became more marked until the Emperor Constantine befriended the new faith and took over. Then, in the words of one historian, "the cross suddenly passed from the scenes of public executions to the diadem of the Caesars. The blood of the martyrs—the seed of the church—ceased to flow, and Christianity became the religion of the State by adoption." From this period on through the Middle and Dark Ages, the early rain diminished from a mighty and universal downpour into periodic effusions, which persisted right up to the beginning of the twentieth century.

In the wondrous glory of the great redemptive plan,

the student will observe the startling and soul-entrancing fact that Jehovah took the land of Canaan to adumbrate the Spirit-filled life, and His methods to supply the needs of that land in the physical are a type of His dealings with His people down to the end of the church dispensation. Jehovah promised His people that if they would obey Him and walk in His statutes and judgments He would water their land, and there would be no need of irrigation, but it would be a land watered by the clouds of heaven (Deuteronomy 11:10-12). Jehovah promised that the rain would fall in season and they would have abundant crops. In His announced program, the "early rain" was to fall after the seed was sown, and there would be periodic showers afterwards as the grain matured. Then the "latter rain" would fall—a veritable deluge—in time to fully develop the grain and assure an abundant harvest.

This is precisely what we have had in the spiritual analogy.[1] We surely received the "early rain" at Pentecost. That was the seed sowing, and it lasted dispensationally for two hundred years, then declined into periodic showers of blessing, which substantiated God's promise and assured His saints that He had not forgotten His holy covenant.

So many tabulations, fully reliable, have been made to emphasize this fact in history that one cannot tabulate without the risk of much repetition. However, history is public property, and we wish to show that the showers in between the early and latter rain in the form of real Pentecostal revivals have dotted the pages of history from the close of the second century until the present time.

Irenaeus was a disciple of the patriarch Polycarp.

This man was a disciple of the apostle John. He wrote many remarkable things to substantiate the thesis herein advocated, but for brevity's sake we append only the following: "We hear many brethren who have prophetic gifts, and they speak in all sorts of languages through the Spirit."

Tertullian carries us over into the middle of the second century and speaks of the spiritual gifts, especially the operation of the power to speak in strange tongues.

Justin Martyr, who lived in this same century, tells how the gifts of the Spirit were in operation in his day (*Smith's Bible Dictionary*, vol. 4, page 3310).

A remarkable passage is culled from the writings of Origen, who died towards the end of the second century: "I suppose that he [Paul] was made debtor to different nations, because through the grace of the Holy Spirit, he had received the gift of speaking in the languages of all the nations; as he, himself, also saith: 'I thank my God I speak with tongues more than ye all.' Since then, anyone receives the knowledge of languages, not for himself but for their sake to whom the gospel is to be preached, he is made debtor to all those of whose languages he received the knowledge from God."

Another significant passage is credited to the great Augustine in the fourth century: "We still do what the apostles did when they laid hands on the Samaritans and called down the Spirit on them by the laying on of the hands. It is expected that the converts should speak with new tongues."[2]

Chrysostom carried the record into the fifth century. He wrote: "Whosoever was baptized in apostolic days, he straightway spoke with tongues . . . the one straightway spoke in the Persian language, another in the Roman, another in the Indian, and another in some other tongue, and this made manifest to them that were without that it was the Spirit in the person speaking."

The church passed through the Middle and the Dark Ages, and it can be ascertained that all the way through the Lord raised up witnesses who were consecrated enough to receive the Holy Spirit with the early sign of speaking in new tongues. Even in the fifteenth century there were revivals in southern Europe in which many spoke with new tongues. This miraculous manifestation was common among the Waldenses and Albigenses.

The Encyclopedia Brittanica is credited with being fully reliable, and it states that the speaking with new tongues occurs in Christian revivals of every age, e.g., among the mendicant friars of the thirteenth century, among the Jensenists and early Quakers, the converts of Wesley and Whitefield, the persecuted Protestants of the Cevennes, and the Irvingites (vol. 27, pages 9-10, 11th edition).

In the famous church history by Philip Schaff, it is related of Vincent Ferrer, who died in 1419, "Spindamus and many others say that this saint was honored with the gift of tongues. This book also tells of Francis Xavier, who died in 1552, that he is said to have been understood by the Hindus without learning their language." The *Catholic Encyclopedia* also speaks of his preaching in tongues unknown to him. Xavier was a deeply spiritual saint and a remarkably successful missionary.

Writing of the revivals among the Huguenots, Pastor A. A. Boddy says: "When Louis XIV of France in 1685 revoked the edict of Nantes which had given religious liberty, he strove by dragonades to drive Protestants into the Roman Catholic Church. The Huguenots were led by John Cavalier, a farmer, into inaccessible mountain passes. Among these persecuted people were those who spoke in new tongues. There exist records given both by enemies and by friends about their prophetic gifts."

In 1862, J. J. Gorres wrote: "The gift which the apostles received on the Day of Pentecost we find in force among the Hermits of the desert. It is related of St. Pachomius, who, wishing to speak with a brother who knew only the Roman language, of which he, himself, was ignorant, received the power to speak the language after praying three hours. This gift is reproduced often in modern times. Ange Clarenus received the gift of speaking in the Greek language. It is related in the *Life of St. Dominick* that this saint, going from Toulon to Paris with his brother, Bertrand, was joined by some Germans travelling the same road. He set himself to pray, and immediately commenced to converse to these Germans in their own language to their utter astonishment. Four whole days he discoursed with them about the Lord Jesus Christ.

"This gift was also accorded to St. Stephen in his missions in Gorgia, so that he spoke Greek, Turkish, and Armenian so fluently that the natives held him in admiration."

In this same book is recorded the fact that Louis Bertrand, who lived from 1526 to 1581, was the recipient of the gift of tongues, of prophecy, and of miracles. It is said that inside three years he converted 30,000 Indians of various tribes and dialects in South America.

In the year 1800, at Saltcoats, on the west coast of

Scotland, twin brothers were born, James and George MacDonald. In the year 1830, both of these brothers were filled with the Holy Spirit. James was the first to receive the Holy Spirit. His sister was apparently in a dying condition, yet so filled at times with the glory that it seemed as if her own weakness had been supplanted by the power and strength of the Holy Spirit. It was while she was in this condition that she prayed that James might be empowered with the Holy Spirit. Almost instantly James calmly said, "I have it!" The first thing he did was to bid his sister rise from the bed, and she did, being completely healed. A few evenings after the above occurrence, during a prayer meeting, George, in whom nothing supernatural had ever previously appeared and whose natural caution had made him the last of the family to welcome the supernatural in others, began suddenly to speak in an unknown tongue. James followed him, and thus commenced that speaking with tongues and prophesying, which never afterwards wholly ceased.

At the time that these brothers received the Holy Spirit with the signs following, others in Scotland received a like experience. In the *Religious Anecdotes of Scotland*, edited by William Adamson and published in 1893, we read the following: "The intensely devoted and pious Mary Campbell of Gareloch fame, lived in Fernicarry, and was the subject of supernatural experiences in the year 1830. These experiences excited great interest in western Scotland. She, with many others, believed that the gift of tongues and other gifts were given to the church, never to be revoked during the entire church age. On a Sunday evening in the month of March, Mary, in the presence of a few friends, began to utter sounds to them incomprehensible, and believed to be tongues such as were spoken on the Day of Pentecost."

The MacDonalds were contemporaries of Edward Irving. In the year 1835, at a time when the Edward Irving church was moving away from its original moorings, George MacDonald wrote to a friend: "At its commencement the work bore every scriptural mark which could be desired as far as we know, and the Spirit of God among ourselves bore abundant testimony to their having received the Holy Spirit among them." This is a testimony to the fact that at its inception Mr. Irving's church really was endowed with the power of the Holy Spirit.

Some years ago, Dr. F. B. Meyer visited Estonia, one of the Baltic provinces of Russia, where he found some simple, peasant congregations of Baptists. He wrote to the London Christians of this wonderful work of the Holy Spirit. He stated, "It is very remarkable when the Lutheran Church of this land has lost its evangelistic fervor, and is inclined to substitute forms and rites for the living power of Christ, that God raised up a devoted nobleman, Baron Uxhull, to preach the gospel with all its simplicity, and is renewing among the peasantry those marvelous manifestations which attended the first preaching of the gospel, when God bore witness to the message of salvation 'with signs and wonders and gifts of the Holy Spirit.' To have come across a movement like this is intensely interesting. The gift of tongues are heard often in these meetings, especially in the villages. They are interpreted to say 'Jesus is coming soon,' or 'Jesus is near.' When these are given, unbelievers in the audience are put under conviction. A gentleman who was present on one of these occasions was deeply impressed by the fact that those who spoke were quite ordinary people until they were uplifted as it were by a trance and then they spoke with so much fluency and refinement."

H. L. Christopher of New Britain, Connecticut, writes of a remarkable revival that the Lord gave in Oslo, Norway, in 1899, in which many Norwegians were filled with the Spirit and spoke with tongues as the Spirit gave them utterance.

This brings us up to the beginnings of the worldwide revival that struck the cities of America in the beginning of the twentieth century and spread all over Christendom. The voice of history leaves no doubt, if examined by impartial judgment, that the words the apostle Peter used in connection with the identity of the Pentecostal phenomenon and the prophecy of Joel— "This Is That"—may be applied with equal consistency and plausibility in regard to the identity of this great worldwide, spiritual awakening with that of Pentecost.

The recipients of the Holy Spirit in the early days of this great spiritual awakening would sing: "I'm glad that the promised Pentecost has come and the latter rain is falling on some. Pour it out, O Lord, upon the thirsty ground till it reaches all the world around." They believed that this outpouring was the real counterpart of the "early rain." That belief still maintains among a majority at the present time.

ENDNOTES

[1]This "latter rain" motif and interpretation of the history of the church can be seen in the writings of most early Pentecostals. In adopting this explanation of the Pentecostal renewal, they merged it with the teaching of dispensationalism that was taught by many Protestants, including those in the Holiness movement.

[2]It seems that this example is erroneous, since in context Augustine apparently stated that people in his day no longer expected to see such miraculous occurrences.

CHAPTER THREE

The Challenge of Pentecost

When Pentecost invaded the modern church, it was regarded as a unique religious unit. Any other movement that had arrested attention had originated within some other organization and appealed to a new interpretation of the Scriptures as justification for its prestige. This sprang from no denomination. It was outside all of them.

This new movement was based entirely on an experience, which had no doctrinal affiliation in modern theology. We search church history for something exactly like it, in vain, until we arrive back at the dawn of the third century of the Christian era.

When Pentecost rocked the religious world with a worldwide spiritual awakening that struck at Los Angeles in 1906, an earthquake of frightful dimensions rocked the physical world, centering in San Francisco. In all of God's great moves, nature sympathizes with Him. She understands whether man does or not. At Sinai, when God spoke, the earth went into convulsions. At Calvary the bosom of the earth rocked violently, the sun withdrew its face, and all nature went into eclipse.

The physical earthquake of San Francisco caused many to lose their property and leave their comfortable homes, where they had lived in comfort and luxury for years. The spiritual earthquake robbed many of their comfortable church homes. These took joyfully the spoiling of their goods. They estimated this spiritual birthright as being of inestimable value. They were willing to sever delicate and tender ties of long denominational standing. The treatment meted out to them in many cases was only paralleled by those who broke with Judaism because of the "better thing" called the gift of the Holy Spirit. History again repeated itself, the identifying marks being speaking with other tongues as the Spirit gave utterance, miraculous gifts of healings, and working of miracles, even to raising the dead, which turned the world upside down.

The religious phenomenon is now (1947) over forty years old and has developed into a preponderating power in the Christian world. Its inescapable challenge to modern Christendom lies in its proximity to the faith of the apostles in precept and practice. In 1906, as at the original Pentecostal effusion, the great burning question was, "What meaneth this?" (Acts 2:12). The answer to this question was substantially identical with that given by Peter on the Day of Pentecost. It was appraised as eminently scriptural, and the joyful slogan among the recipients of this experience was, "This Is That!" (See Acts 2:16.) This slogan or greeting among the saints was not based on any doctrinal imputation, but the identical, supernatural ecstasy that thrilled the hearts of the first recipients of this marvelous experience. The speaking with a new language became the one outstanding physical manifestation that drew the hottest fire of the enemy. The "New Thing" became a second Jonah. It could be swallowed but not assimilated.

It may be admitted that many of its advocates placed an undue emphasis on speaking with other tongues. Naturally, the truth centralized in an outward, immediate sign can become distorted. It is possible to misplace the emphasis and make more of the mere sign than the supreme fact of becoming filled with the Spirit of God.

However, it was the definite, tangible, glorious experience of being filled with God's Spirit that made Pentecost so real. It transcended all theological wrangling about correct doctrine. It brought Jesus the Christ out of the hurly-burly of speculation into human hearts and lives to become the living, thrilling, potent reality to heal their diseases, quicken their sensibilities, illuminate their minds, help bear their burdens, dry their tears, solve their problems, and fight their battles. The central fact of redemption—"Christ in you, the hope of glory"—comes through the experience of the baptism with the Holy Spirit, as received on and after the Day of Pentecost.

It was this exact experience that brought thousands out of their churches to form the present Pentecostal movement; out of their worldliness, formality, lukewarmness, and halfheartedness into a worldwide spiritual fellowship that overcame all distinctions of race, creed, or class. The rich man shouted and sobbed with the outcast and the servant. The heavenly chorus, sung by Spirit-inspired people with shining faces; the experimental testimonies, which amounted to a miracle in words; the supernatural presence of the Lord prevading throughout the meeting and sometimes lasting clear into the morning hours—these were the factors that made personal participation in Pentecost the one overmastering, all-absorbing passion of the onlookers. Soul hunger after this experience became intolerable to many who, for reasons known only to God and themselves, tarried for weeks and even months without a letup in order to obtain this "like precious faith."

This palpable identification of the effect of the "early rain" and the "latter rain" upon the recipients coupled the early faith once delivered with the latter faith again restored in all its fruitfulness, power, and glory.

Another striking point of our proximity to the apostolic faith is the special and inveterate persecution hurled against it. The earmark of the early faith is expressed in the closing verses of the Acts of the Apostles: "For as concerning this sect, we know that every where it is spoken against" (Acts 28:22). Our aggressive preachers have been imprisoned in many states of this union for preaching their experiences and convictions. They never resorted to carnal weapons, which linked them with the apostles and early martyrs. The writer has been mobbed, stoned, rotten-egged, and imprisoned for his open proclamation of soul convictions; he is now nearing the seventy-year mark. He received this wonderful experience in 1908 and has been at the head of a Pentecostal work ever since. The heart-rending thing about this horrible fact is that, as it was in the early church, the religious leaders have contributed most of the persecution.

Another very significant point of our proximity to the early church is that most of this persecution came because of good deeds being done in the name of Jesus for the needy, for sick folk, for cripples, and for people with incurable diseases of every description. It was because Peter and John were used to heal the impotent man in Jerusalem that they received floggings and imprisonment. When the nominal churches are powerless to heal the sick or pray the revolutionizing prayer of faith, they are stung to their hearts with conviction when another unimposing church preaches the Word with the signs following. Persecution is the inevitable result. We have had the same identical performance as is described in the third chapter of the Acts of the Apostles, only lawless mobs administered the cruel floggings and were not apprehended.

Another point of identification between the early and latter church is the marvelous zeal for soul saving, both at home and abroad. Our missionaries have covered most of the known missionary fields in the world and are still going forth to conquer new fields in the all-prevailing name of Jesus. The money that is contributed yearly for missionary enterprise is simply astounding. In one of the writer's pastorates, for eight years we contributed a thousand dollars a month, and sometimes to meet a special need two thousand dollars would be raised. This is being duplicated in many of our larger churches today.

The theology of both the "early rain" and "latter rain" recipients was inseparably linked with their experiences. We believe that "God is one," and we demonstrate our faith by getting results in prayer to that one Lord in the name of Jesus. Whatsoever we do, we are careful to do in the name of Jesus. This simple faith in the efficacy of the name of the Lord Jesus Christ has turned the religious world upside down as it did in the days of the "early rain." We do not trouble our souls when higher critics inform us that Mark 16:17-18 is not in the earliest Greek manuscripts. With an unswerving faith in the inerrancy of God's Word, the truth is demonstrated and these five signs are in evidence in our ministrations.

This then is the supreme challenge of Pentecost among the modern churches of Christendom. In raising up this witness for His Word, God has jumped back over the centuries, beyond Dr. Simpson, John Wesley, Madam Guyon, Luther, the Dark Ages, clear back to the first century. This movement is a burning protest against worldliness, formality, and deadness in religious worship. It indicts every church that teaches that the miracles and signs of the early church cannot be repeated. It demonstrates to the world that Christianity is not in word but in power, that all the promises of God are yea and amen in Christ Jesus.

Acting on an unswerving faith that the Word of God is demonstrable today, during these last forty years literally thousands of people have been healed of incurable diseases. Doctors have been completely confounded when, after pronouncing their verdict that their patients would die in a short time, they found them apparently well. Many honest physicians have confessed that their patients were healed by divine power.

The gifts are also in evidence: the gifts of prophecy, tongues, interpretation of tongues and working of miracles. These things have made it possible to present to the world a ministry sustained by signs and miracles and gifts of the Holy Ghost. People are still confounded as they were back in the early church and ask in amazement: "What meaneth this?"

Christianity without Pentecost is impossible. In fact, it is an absurdity. It is not Christianity; it is churchanity. No religious fellowship can enter into that which Pentecost stands for unless it presses into a deep and profound experience of the baptism of fire. Without that, Pentecost as we have it today would soon be an emaciated remembrance. Let us maintain our burning testimony for the truth and go on unto perfection. God gave this experience in the beginning of the church. It was accompanied with tongues, manifestations of the Spirit, a heavenly ecstasy, and a consecration unto death. That same God says: "I am Jehovah; I change not!"

CHAPTER FOUR

The Revival in Topeka, Kansas

When Charles F. Parham dedicated a building for the Lord's work, henceforth to be known as the Bethel Bible School, in the year 1900, he unconsciously prepared the birthplace of the most startling religious phenomenon of modern times.

This building was known to the people of Topeka, Kansas, as "Stone's Folly." The reason was that it had been patterned after an English castle, but the builder, not having counted the cost, was unable to finish it according to the original blueprint. The best obtainable data featured the beautiful carved stairwork of cedar, spotted pine, cherry wood, and bird's eye maple. However, this ended at the third floor with plain pine and common maple.

Oddly enough, there was a cupola at the rear of the

building on the top, built in with two domes on either side. Into one of these a door was cut, making a room large enough for a prayer tower. After the Bible school was established, volunteers from among the students took their turn of a three-hour watch so that day and night prayer was ascending unto God.

About forty persons assembled in this building for Bible study. Their adopted method was to select a subject, find all the references on it, and present to the class a scriptural summary of what the Scriptures had to say about the theme.

Just before the new year, the classes decided to take up the study of the baptism with the Holy Ghost. Mr. Parham was about to visit Kansas City, and before he went he told the students that he was familiar with all the leading teachers' theories about the baptism with the Holy Ghost and the various evidences that one had received it. He said that not one of these theories entirely satisfied him. "Now, students," he said, "while I am gone, search the Scriptures to see if you can find some sign or evidence that is outstanding in apostolic precepts and practices in the reception of this vital experience, the baptism with the Holy Ghost."

On Mr. Parham's return, he immediately assembled the students and asked them whether they had found any real outstanding Bible evidence of the baptism with the Holy Ghost. The answer was unanimous: "speaking in other tongues as the Spirit gave utterance."

Meetings followed daily and each night. People were intensely expectant and hungry for the scriptural experience of the gift of the Holy Ghost. There seemed to be a hallowed hush over the entire building, and all felt the influence of the supernatural presence in their midst. Mr. Parham was amazed at the harmony that prevailed and was heard to exclaim, "Truly, the Lord is with us and has something for us such as we have not known before."

At the entering into the new year, it came. The watch-night service was especially spiritual, and every heart seemed hungry for the whole will of God to be wrought in them. The first to receive the gift of the Holy Spirit in the full scriptural order was Agnes Ozman LaBerge, a student in the Bible school. We are privileged to report the great event in her own words: "As the end of the year drew near, some friends came from Kansas City to spend the holidays with us. On watchnight we had a most blessed service, praying that God's blessing might rest upon us as the new year came in. During the first day of 1901, the presence and power of the Lord was with us in a marked way, encouraging our hearts to wait upon Him for greater things. The spirit of prayer was upon us in the evening.

"It was nearly seven o'clock on this first day of January that it came into my heart to ask Brother Parham to lay his hands on me that I might receive the Holy Ghost. Instantly, the Holy Spirit came upon me and I began to speak in other tongues and to glorify God. I talked several languages, and it was clearly manifest when a new language was spoken. I had the added joy and glory my heart had longed for and a depth of the presence of the Lord such as no tongue can describe. It was the fulfillment of the promise of the Master: 'He that believeth on me, as the scripture hath said, out of his belly shall flow rivers of living water.'" (See John 7:38.)

When this innovation became known, the old Bible

school became the most popular building in Topeka. Hundreds flocked to see the great sight. Prayer was held day and night, and soon the experience of Acts 2:4 was duplicated in hundreds of cases. Brother Parham received it, and was turned into a living, moving witness of God's miraculous power and glory. Nearly every hungry soul he laid his hand on in the name of Jesus was satisfied by having his great heart hunger relieved. The signs of apostolic power were in evidence everywhere. The people of Topeka became sensible of the presence and power of the Deity in their midst.

The fire quickly spread to Kansas City, Lawrence, Galena, Melrose, Keelville, and Baxter Springs. When the fire would reach a city or town, Brother Parham and his workers would follow up, and renting the largest building obtainable, they would hold a revival meeting. Sometimes, as at Galena and Baxter Springs, no building could hold the crowds, and they would pitch a tent in a convenient location and carry on for months.

As the heralds of this new message went from place to place, it seemed impossible that any normal soul could resist the evidence of the power and glory of God. Some of the messages in tongues were irresistible, and in almost every place some would understand the languages spoken and get convicted. It was Pentecost being repeated: "How hear we every man in our own tongue, wherein we were born? . . . We do hear them speak in our own tongues the wonderful works of God" (Acts 2:8, 11). But with the majority the prophecy was fulfilled: "With men of other tongues and other lips will I speak unto this people; yet for all that will they not hear me, saith the Lord" (I Corinthians 14:21).

At the great meeting in Baxter Springs, the sick were brought from hundreds of miles away, and in every case where they believed, miracles of healing would take place. It is reported that everything they had in the early Christian church was in evidence, and many were heard to exclaim that Pentecost was literally being repeated in every meeting.

Soon after the revival in Topeka, ministers of the gospel began to inquire after this new way, and many of the more noble who searched the Scriptures and found that the experience was scriptural became seekers at the altars. Many were filled with the Holy Ghost, speaking with other tongues, and joined Brother Parham in his vigorous crusades.

When the Pentecostal fire struck and centered in Houston, the great metropolis of the South, a basis was established from whence eventually it was to spread to the uttermost parts of the earth. The story we have from a venerable elder, who was a prominent figure in Pentecostal work throughout the South, reads like a chapter from the Book of Acts. After the revival in Brunner, the fire spread rapidly through the South, and eventually Houston became the headquarters of the Apostolic Faith Movement, as it was then known.

One of the most remarkable coincidences is related about a band of ministers and saints who had boarded a train at Orchard, Texas.[1] Many were sad-hearted at not having yet received the baptism with the Holy Ghost when so many others had received; and as they all flocked into the same car and got settled, Brother Parham, who had boarded the train to ride with them as far as the next station, came into the car smiling and praising the Lord. As he took the hand of one of the disappointed shop boys from Houston, the Spirit fell on the boy and he began to speak in other tongues, blessing and praising God. By the time they arrived at Alvin, no less than ten had received the baptism, speaking in other tongues. We have it from the best authority that our beloved Brother Howard A. Goss, who is now the superintendent of the United Pentecostal Church, received his baptism on this train.[2] Many other ministers received and went to work for God and righteousness with the real Pentecostal equipment. Some have passed on, but others are alive and still remain in the ranks of Holy Ghost-filled ministers, preaching the good tidings of the kingdom of God.

One of the greatest revivals in the history of the Christian church started. The fire spread to Chicago and from there to Zion City, where two thousand were converted to the new faith. From there it went to New York City. Ministers were attracted to these famous central cities from all parts of the world and, on returning to their churches, spread the good news. Revival fires sprang up everywhere.

We have reports from Elders W. F. Carothers and T. M. Bowen about those wonderful days of blessing and power. On the basis of true apostolic unity that prevailed, it seemed that both the heathen and denominational world would be enveloped in the irresistible sweep of this revival. The influx was wholesale during these first few years. Whole congregations and whole movements accepted the message and were baptized in the Holy Spirit, speaking with other tongues. It seemed that there was little need to tarry in order to receive the Holy Spirit baptism in those wonderful days; rather the order was that which prevailed on and after the Day of Pentecost when all that heard the word were baptized and were added to the church by the baptism with the Spirit, speaking with other tongues and prophesying. Division came over doctrine, and the power began to diminish, but not until the faith once delivered to the saints was firmly established. The fire spread from Houston to Los Angeles, and from Los Angeles it went to every corner of Christendom.

The division was caused over divergent views regarding the unity of the Deity and the mode of Christian baptism. We have it from the pen of our esteemed Brother W. F. Carothers that, in order to maintain the unity of the Spirit until we all come into the unity of the faith and preserve the great movement intact, he advised not to make doctrine a basis of fellowship, but to have an association based on the baptism with the Holy Spirit, speaking with other tongues. He said that all the main brethren, such as E. N. Bell, J. W. Welch, and A. P. Collins—in fact, all the council brethren in the South and Middle West—agreed. However, Brother Brown and his group from New York prevailed upon the council to adopt a 27-point creed and demanded its acceptance by all who wished to remain in fellowship with them.[3] Elder Carothers believed the 27-point creed, but because they broke faith and seceded from the first agreement, he withdrew and handed in his credentials. He said that in his judgment this action turned the council into a sect, and is plainly condemned by Scripture. Because of this, the Oneness people, who had grown into a great imposing company, were forced to withdraw.

The writer is trying hard to assume the viewpoint of

the historian in the authorship of this book; however, because he is widely known as the ringleader of the Oneness crowd, and believes that the revelation regarding God and His name is absolutely fundamental to participation in the faith of the early apostles—the "faith which was once delivered unto the saints" (Jude 3)—his job is rather difficult and most unenviable.

After all, ever since the immortal and intrepid Luther received the great revelation of justification by faith and walked out of the Roman Catholic Church in order to proclaim it, the same procedure has been repeated by those whom God gave a revelation of new truth.

We heard of the baptism with the Holy Ghost according to Acts 2:4; we accepted it, and through our very acceptance we became a separate unit in the religious world. When Brother Durham preached his message of "the finished work of Calvary," history repeated itself, and indeed there are imposing congregations of Pentecostal people today who cling tenaciously to the former theory of a "second, definite, instantaneous work of grace" as true, scriptural sanctification. If there is another way to get back the pure faith of the apostles, which consisted of a definite system of doctrine, we have no example of it.

No one can truthfully say that we, as a body of Pentecostal people, left the main body of our own free choice. We were refused fellowship of our brethren on the basis of our new beliefs.

How the apostolic fellowship and unity is to be restored, we do not know. But we read in the Scriptures that it will be in the end time. We realize our sacred obligations to earnestly strive to maintain the unity of the

Spirit till we all come into the unity of the faith. This sacred obligation may lead one saint to do things that another saint feels that he cannot honestly do and be true to his convictions. Many saints have been stigmatized as compromisers who are not guilty of the charge.

If it were possible to create a fellowship based entirely on the experience of the baptism of the Holy Spirit, which made us members of the same body, and independent of the unity of doctrine, and maintain the divine approval, that is what we all want. The dilemma is to reconcile such a basis of fellowship with that of the apostles and the early fathers. It is written that the early church "continued stedfastly in the apostles' doctrine and fellowship, and in breaking of bread, and in prayers" (Acts 2:42).

The writer's prayer is that each reader of this history will try to imbibe the lessons of history, making steppingstones of our past experiences to rise to higher heights of holiness and glory and attainment in our blessed Lord. Amen.

ENDNOTES

[1]Apparently Ewart's primary source for this account is *The Life of Charles Parham*, 143-44. Howard Goss also related this event in *The Winds of God*. He told of his receiving the Spirit and reported that twelve people in his coach and five in another received the Holy Ghost between Orchard and Alvin. After his group changed trains at Alvin to go to Angleton, five more people received the Holy Ghost, making a total of twenty-two filled with the Spirit on the train.

[2]Howard Goss served as the general superintendent of the United Pentecostal Church from 1945 to 1951.

[3]Ewart's reference is to the Statement of Fundamental Truths, adopted at the Fourth General Council of the Assemblies of God, October 1916. The statement had sixteen sections.

CHAPTER FIVE

The Azusa Street Revival

In the year 1906, one of our most disastrous earthquakes struck and centered in the city of San Francisco, California, and almost simultaneously the greatest revival of modern time struck and centered in the city of Los Angeles. In many respects the effects in the natural and spiritual world were similar. In the earthquake the many who were spared lost their homes. In the spiritual earthquake those who participated lost their spiritual homes. The new revival was a sort of nondescript in the religious world. It could not fit in with any known denomination. It was not built on a system of new doctrine but on an eminent scriptural experience. However, because it had not been popular in the religious world since the dawn of the third century, it was decidedly in the discard.

Brother W. J. Seymour was born in Louisiana. He was

saved and sanctified under the teaching of "The Evening Lights Saints." He, like millions of others, believed like he was taught and acted on that belief. He was a colored man, blind in one eye.[1] He was a very humble and spiritually minded brother. His sweet winsomeness broke down the barriers erected by doctrinal bigotry and won people's trust and love, despite their previous animosities.

He had heard about the wonderful Holy Ghost revival in the South and one day happened to meet a Sister Farrow of Houston, Texas. He had actually acted as pastor at the Holiness Mission in Houston while she went to Kansas to help Parham. When she returned from Kansas, he was astonished to learn that the Apostolic Faith Movement, after thorough investigation of the Scriptures, taught that though there were other evidences of one's receiving the real baptism of the Holy Spirit with the Bible earmark, the speaking in other tongues as the Holy Spirit gave utterance was "the evidence"! He was amazed because he had thought like millions of others that one received the Holy Spirit in sanctification. However, when Sister Farrow, in whom he had implicit confidence, assured him that she was so hungry for the blessed and holy experience that she threw all anxious care about correct doctrine to the wind and began seeking God to satisfy her hungry soul, knowing that He had promised that if we ask bread He would not give us a stone, and that she received an experience that duplicated Acts 2:4, he was convinced.

The preacher then began to seek the Lord, through much heart-searching and study of the Word. The faithful Holy Spirit, who leads every honest heart into full possession of the truth, showed him that he was wrong about being baptized in the Holy Spirit. He had received a great blessing and had named it sanctification, according to the teaching he had received.

Brother Seymour then began to ask God to empty his heart and mind of every false idea regarding what the Bible teaches, and it was then that the Lord made plain Acts 2:4, as the personal experience, and subsequent to all other blessings.

It happened that a sister in the Lord from Los Angeles who was affiliated with a small, colored Nazarene church, visited with friends in Houston, Texas. She, like many others, came under the sway of Brother Seymour's gripping personality. On her return to Los Angeles she told the saints about a "very godly and humble man" she had met in Houston. At once these colored saints sent an invitation to this preacher to come and hold a meeting for them. In due time he arrived. The first Sunday morning he took Acts 2:4 for his text in that Nazarene church pulpit. The saints were dumbfounded. They never heard such a sermon before, and never expected it. He said that when anyone received the baptism with the Holy Spirit according to the original pattern, he would have the identical experience with that which the disciples received on the Day of Pentecost, and speak with new tongues just as they did on that occasion.

When the meeting was dismissed, Brother Lee, a much esteemed colored saint who was a member of the Peniel Mission, invited Brother Seymour to his home to take dinner. When they returned to the mission for the afternoon service, the door was locked. Brother Seymour asked the reason for this and was told that he was judged to be a preacher of an utterly false doctrine. They would not permit him to preach in their pulpit anymore. So Brother Lee, solely out of Christian courtesy towards the visiting preacher and not that he believed in his doctrine, invited him to his home. Brother Seymour had no place to live, and Brother Lee felt that he could not leave the stranger homeless while he had a home. The saints who had invited Brother Seymour left him stranded without any money to return to Houston. Brother Seymour stayed in his room and prayed. Brother and Sister Lee did not feel good towards him, but they could not find it in their hearts to command him to leave. They had an unwelcome guest on their hands.

After a few nights in the home, Brother Seymour asked them if they would join him in prayer when Brother Lee would return from his daily work. This they did, and immediately the Spirit of God began to take hold of their hearts, and the hosts felt differently towards their preacher guest. In a few days the saints from the little church began to come around to learn whether the stranger was still in town.

They found such a wonderful spirit of prayer in that home that they also began to humble themselves before the Lord. The Lord would impress everyone who came to that home with the necessity of seeking His face in prayer. The spirit of conviction seized every true saint, no matter how they believed, and they would fall on their knees and confess that God was in that place. They would not receive this praying man's doctrine, but they loved to be near him and to pray with him.

Then came a new innovation. A Baptist, Sister Asbury, came in and invited Brother Seymour and as many as were hungry for more of God to hold the prayer meeting in her home. So they began the protracted prayer meetings in the home of Brother and Sister Asbury at 214 North Bonnie Brae Street. These hungry souls tarried day and night, and in the meantime the Spirit of the Lord had inspired Brother Lee so that he was in constant prayer. He was a janitor in the bank at Seventh and Spring Streets for years. He said that he used to go down into the basement of the bank and hide away for hours and hours in deep, heart-searching meditation and prayer.

One day the Lord gave him a vision. He plainly saw two men come to him, and he was impressed that they were Peter and John. He said that he was not asleep but, like Peter on the housetop, had fallen into a trance. They stood and looked down on him; then they lifted their hands toward heaven and shook mightily under the power of God and spoke in other tongues. He said that he jumped up to apprehend them and to ask them some questions, but they vanished. Brother Lee said that he shook from head to feet under the power of God. When he went home that night, he said to Brother Seymour, "I know now how people act when they get the power of the Holy Ghost." Brother Seymour had previously explained the manifestations of the Spirit to the group, but it had sounded like idle tales and they could not understand it. Brother Seymour could not impress the people, but after Brother Lee had his vision a deeper hunger was stirred in his heart, and when he related it, the saints began to believe that he had outlined a real scriptural experience. Brother Lee began to seek more earnestly than ever for the baptism.

One evening he came in from his work and said to

Brother Seymour, "If you will lay hands on me I will receive my baptism!" But Brother Seymour said, "No, the Lord wants me to lay hands suddenly on no man." Later on in the evening, however, Brother Seymour approached Brother Lee and said, "Brother, I lay my hands on you in Jesus' name!" Immediately Brother Lee fell under the mighty power of God as though he were dead. Sister Lee was so frightened that she began to scream and cry, "What have you done to my husband?"

In a few minutes Brother Lee rose up and sat in his chair. Brother Seymour said afterwards that he prayed and asked the Lord to let him get right up as they all seemed so scared, and the Lord could not finish the work at that time. Brother Lee had a wonderful blessing which was the prelude to a mighty baptism in the Spirit. After a time Sister Farrow arrived from Texas, and Brother Lee asked her to lay hands on him. She did and the same thing happened; he dropped as one dead out of his chair, but this time he began to speak in other tongues. He only spoke a few words in tongues and got up. This puzzled Sister Lee and her brother, and they asked if that was all there was to a full and complete baptism. Brother Seymour told them that there was only one baptism but many fillings, and that Brother Lee would have lots of manifestations from this day forward.

They went on over to the prayer meeting in Sister Asbury's home. When Brother Lee walked into the house, he threw up his hands and began to speak in other tongues. Six people were already on their knees praying, and the power fell on them and all six began to speak in tongues as the Spirit gave them utterance. This happened on April 9, 1906. This was followed, as at Pentecost, by a great noise that was spread abroad.

The new recipients were beside themselves with joy. They shouted and praised God for three days and nights. It was the Easter season. The people came from everywhere. By the next morning there was no way of getting near that house. Those who could gain an entrance would fall under God's power as they entered and commence to speak in other tongues; and this continued until the whole city of Los Angeles was mightily stirred. The vibrations of their voices raised to God in praise until the house shook violently as though by an earthquake. The foundations of the house were impaired, but no one was hurt. Then they prayed the prayer of the apostles of old: "Lord, . . . grant unto thy servants, that with all boldness they may speak thy word, by stretching forth thine hand to heal; and that signs and wonders may be done by the name of thy holy child Jesus" (Acts 4:29-30).

During these three wonderful days hundreds of people were saved, the sick were healed, and many received the baptism with the Holy Ghost according to the scriptural pattern.[2] Then they went out to find themselves a church home. They were led to an idle building on Azusa Street. It had been used for a Methodist church. It was an old frame building of two stories. It had been converted in part for a tenement house, having a large, unfurnished, barnlike room on the lower floor. It was in the vicinity of a tombstone shop, and some stables and a lumberyard were nearby, so that no one would be likely to complain about all-night meetings. The accommodations for their first meeting were some planks laid across empty nail kegs so as to seat about thirty people. All racial distinctions were broken down in this first gathering, as colored and white sat together. Thus started the great worldwide revival that attracted people from all parts of the earth.

That meeting lasted for about three years, going on day and night without a break. The writer has contacted many of the preachers and workers at Azusa Street in those early days. The news spread far and wide that Los Angeles had been visited by a sweeping revival after the order of that which struck the world on the Day of Pentecost. The conditions that are counted necessary for a real revival were all wanting. No instruments of music were used. None were needed. The choir was substituted by what was called "The Heavenly Choir." This singing service was literally inspired by the Holy Ghost. It was mostly in known tunes, but in words chosen by the Holy Ghost. This was perhaps the most supernatural and amazing thing about the meetings. It was this that convicted the writer that God was in the midst, when he received the baptism two years after this revival.

Bands of angels have been seen by those under the power of the Spirit at such times of heavenly visitation. Here was one choir without a discord. No collections were taken. But eyewitnesses said that Brother Seymour would go around with five- and ten-dollar bills sticking out of his hip pockets, which people had crammed in there unnoticed by him. Brother Glenn A. Cook, who was one of the workers, said that the food would come in from day to day for the upkeep of the workers who lived in the building, but no one inquired as to its source.

God was recognized as the giver of all and received all the glory and praise. No bills were printed to advertise the meetings at the commencement. Neither were there any worldly newspapers patronized. There was no church organization backing of this revival. As soon as one would enter the house he would be impressed with the supernatural atmosphere. One man who was a normal schoolteacher, very well educated but who did not receive the baptism and who according to his own confession had also criticized and mocked the saints, told the writer that when one got within three blocks of the meetinghouse he could feel the atmosphere change, and it got stronger with the supernatural as one approached. He said that when one opened the door and entered the room, he seemed to be ushered into a holy, sequestered place, a veritable "Holy of Holies." All who were in touch with God realized as soon as they entered the meeting that the Holy Ghost was in full control. One preacher stated that when his train was entering the city miles away, he felt the power of the revival. Travelers from lands afar wended their way to the little barnlike structure at 312 Azusa Street, Los Angeles, California. It was the most important address in the great "city of angels," as it was called. When one looked at this building he would never expect heavenly visitations there, unless he remembered Bethlehem's famous manger.

When it was announced that the altar was available for seeking the Lord, people would rise and flock to the front. Altar calls were not needed. No urging was necessary. The pastor, Brother Seymour, would tell the seekers to ask definite petitions of the Lord, according to their needs. Be emphatic! Ask for salvation, sanctification, the baptism in the Holy Ghost, or divine healing for your sickness: on the basis of this clear exhortation, definite, personalized prayers ascended, and they did not pray for anything or everything, and such prayers never went long unanswered. These saints never would sing such songs as we sing now: "God always answers prayer. Sometime, somehow, somewhere!" No, indeed! There was a great inward urge, based on a desperate need, and a personal appropriation of Christ to fill that need at once.

There was such power in the preached Word that people would shake in their seats, and many would have the power fall on them as the Word germinated in their hearts, and they would burst out speaking or singing in other languages. These meetings were entirely devoid of all nationalistic distinctions. If a man could not speak English, he got up and spoke in his own native tongue. He manifested no embarrassment, for the language was interpreted in the faces of the people, who said, "Amen, Brother," and got blessed. No instrument that God could use was rejected on account of color, or dress, or lack of education. This was a very significant factor in the marvelous accumulating power of this revival.

Seekers for healing were usually taken upstairs and prayed for by experienced believers appointed by Brother Seymour for that work. The vast majority of these were healed. There was a large room upstairs that was invariably being used for a Bible study. A brother described it thus: "Upstairs there is a long room furnished with chairs and three California redwood planks laid end to end on backless chairs. This was called the Pentecostal Upper Room, where sanctified souls seek the fullness of the Spirit baptism and go away praising God in other tongues." A Methodist minister said, "I was an assistant in the First Methodist Church. We prayed that the power might fall there, and because it didn't we rejected it."

ENDNOTES

[1]Throughout the book, Ewart speaks of blacks (African Americans) as "colored" or "Negro." In doing so, he used the standard terminology of his time and clearly intended no disparagement. Several times he noted with approval that the Pentecostal experience broke down racial barriers, and he expressed great appreciation for leading black ministers such as W. J. Seymour and G. T. Haywood.

[2]William J. Seymour was one of those filled with the Holy Ghost, receiving the Spirit on April 12, 1906.

CHAPTER SIX

Azusa Street Continued

A four-page, free paper called *The Apostolic Faith* was published from Azusa Street headquarters, and from a copy which we have retained, we quote the following extract: "The waves of Pentecostal salvation are still rolling in Azusa Street Mission. From morning till late at night meetings continue with about three altar services a day. We have made no record of souls saved, sanctified, and baptized in the Holy Spirit, but a brother made a count for one week and there were about fifty in all who had received the baptism with the Holy Ghost. Among this number were four Holiness preachers. One of these, Pastor William Pendleton, and his congregation have been turned out of the church. They are now holding services at Eighth and Maple Streets. There is a heavenly atmosphere there. The altar is continually filled with seekers, people are being slain under the power of the Holy Ghost and are being healed and filled with the Holy Ghost.

"Different nationalities are now hearing the gospel in their own tongue wherein they were born, as at Pentecost. A sister, Anna Hall, spoke to the Russians in their church in Los Angeles in their own language as the Spirit gave utterance. They were so glad to hear the truth that they wept and kissed her hands. They are very poor and simple, but hungry for the full gospel. The other night as a company of Russians were present in the meeting, Brother Lee, a converted Catholic, was permitted to speak their language. As he spoke and sang, one of the Russians came up from the audience and embraced him and called him 'my brother!' It was a holy scene, and the Spirit fell upon the Russians as well as the balance of the audience, and we all glorified God together."

In December 1906, *The Apostolic Faith* was able to report: "Hundreds of souls have received salvation and healing. The Lord God is in Los Angeles, in different missions and churches that have sprung from Azusa Street Mission, and is working in mighty power, despite the bitter opposition that is being manifested. This great revival has spread through suburban towns round about Los Angeles, and will soon cover the entire States of America. The blood of Jesus Christ prevails against every force and power of the enemy. Glory to God!"

An eyewitness writing of those early days in Los Angeles said, "Brother Seymour usually sits behind two empty shoe boxes, one on top of the other. He usually kept his head inside the top one, during the prayer service, and sometimes through most of the meeting. There was no pride there. The services ran almost continuously. Seeking souls could be found under the power almost any hour of the day. People came to Azusa Street to meet God. He was always there, hence the continuous fellowship. God's presence became more and more manifest. In that old building with its low rafters and bare floor, God took strong men and women to pieces, and then put them together again for His glory. It was a tremendous overhauling process. Pride, self-assertion, self-importance, or self-esteem could not survive there.

"There were no special speakers announced, and no sermon themes were ever announced for special occasions. There were no special occasions. The unexpected invariably happened. No one knew what was coming next. What God would do? All was spontaneous, in the freedom of the Spirit. We wanted to hear from God through whom He might speak. There was no room for the proverbial 'Corinthian carnality' with its respect of preachers. Human worship was impossible in that atmosphere. The Spirit dominated the scene. The rich and educated were in the same grade as the poor and ignorant, and found that they had a much deeper death to die. No flesh might glory in His presence. The self-opinionated were not used. Those were Holy Ghost meetings, led of the Lord. All went down in humility together at His feet."

A. H. Post, a Baptist minister of Pasadena, wrote: "About the middle of June, I was led to the meetings at Azusa Street. I was convinced that God was indeed working. At the altar service I quietly presented myself before the Lord. On the second day, while at the altar, as distinctly to my inner consciousness as a clear voice to my ear, the Lord said, 'Receive ye the Holy Ghost.' As a hungry person would readily take food, I eagerly accepted the gift of my Lord. This was Saturday afternoon. On the Monday following I returned to Los Angeles and was in meetings all day. The meeting at night was very remarkable. As Brother Seymour preached, God's power seemed to be increasing in him. Near the close of the sermon, as suddenly as the Day of Pentecost, while I was sitting in front of the preacher the Holy Spirit fell upon me and literally filled me. I shouted and praised the Lord and incidentally I began to speak in other tongues. Two of the saints quite a distance apart saw the Spirit fall upon me. Oh, how God did fill my whole being in a manner indescribable!"

The writer of the above testimony later went to Egypt as a missionary, and God used him especially in the ministry of intercession. As a result of his constant life of prayer, there came a great revival in Egypt, starting in Assiout and spreading throughout the land.

The people from the most spiritual churches in Los Angeles flocked to Azusa Street Mission. Pastors, evangelists, and foreign missionaries came to see the wondrous scenes. It seemed that persons of every nationality were represented. Many of these had no definite experience of salvation, merely church membership, still unregenerate. These would be seized with deep conviction of sin under the burning testimony of one of their own nationality, and would at once yield to the Lord and get real experiences. Often some foreigner would hear a testimony in his own tongue and seek the Lord.

According to the consensus of judgment of an eyewitness, the pastor, W. J. Seymour, did not overemphasize speaking with tongues or manifestations of the Spirit. He would invariably warn the people not to go from the mission and try to get people to come there to hear the saints speak in other languages, rather, to try and get them hungry for real salvation, sanctification, and the infilling of the Spirit according to the Scriptures. He would preach against all unbecoming manifestations and everything not scripturally spiritual. He constantly exalted the atoning work of Christ and the sovereign Word of God. He would earnestly insist on a thorough conversion.

A reporter from one of the daily papers was assigned to write an account of the meetings held by those supposedly ignorant, fanatical, and demented people at Azusa Street Mission. It was to be written from the standpoint of the comic or the ridiculous—the more highly sensational, the better. The reporter went to the meetings with a psychology in fullest harmony with his employers, all alert on doing a popular job. He felt that he was going to a circus under a religious guise. But he witnessed some very touching and solemn scenes: prodigal sons who had got to be desperadoes at an early age were saved and wept out their penitential joy in their mothers' and fathers' arms; crippled men threw away their crutches after being prayed for; and the testimonies of those who were healed of incurable diseases. These things made a terrible impression on him, sobered him up.

Suddenly a Spirit-filled woman gave a mighty, powerful exhortation, an appeal to the sinner to turn to God. Soon she broke out in a language with which she was utterly unfamiliar. It was the native tongue of the foreign-born reporter. Directing her earnest gaze upon him, she poured forth such a holy torrent of truth, exposing his sinful, licentious life, that he was dumbfounded. No one seemingly understood the language but he himself.

When the services were over he at once forced his way to the woman. He asked her if she knew what she had said concerning him while speaking in that particular foreign language. "Not a word," was the prompt reply. At first he could not believe her, but her evident sincerity convinced him that she knew nothing of the language. Then he told her that she had given an entirely true statement of his wicked life, had told things that nobody knew but he, and now he knew that her utterances were from God in order to lead him to repentance and a change of heart. He promised her that he would faithfully follow such a course. He went from the meeting directly to the paper office and informed his employer that he could not give them such a report as they had assigned for him to write. He told them that if they wanted a true and impartial report of the meetings he would gladly write it for them. But his offer was turned down. They did not want that!

R. J. Scott, one of the workers at those early meetings in Azusa Street Mission, told the writer that his little daughter, Kathleen, received the baptism with the Holy Spirit and spoke in several languages. One day a Hebrew scholar came to the meeting, and when the altar call was given he weaved his way to the front, but his conduct was suspected by the workers as he was not seeking the Lord but engaging everyone he could in conversation. Suddenly the power of the Spirit came upon little Kathleen, and she pointed her finger at him and began to pour forth a torrent of strange words. The man was seen to turn pale. He never took his eyes off her, and when she stopped he asked for an audience. Then he told how this little girl had spoken to him in the Hebrew tongue and warned him that he was under the judgment of God and advised him to repent of his sins and change his ways.

One day a poor woman who knew only the English language, and that very imperfectly, left the mission to get some refreshments. While crossing a street she met a Frenchman coming in the opposite direction. She suddenly spoke to him in his native tongue. He stopped abruptly and, with a Frenchman's politeness, asked, "Since when have you been able to speak French?" To this she replied, "I did not know that I spoke French, for I do not understand a word of that language." The man answered, "You certainly spoke in very excellent French. You warned me to repent of my sins and to give my heart and life to God."

S. J. Mead, a missionary who had labored for over twenty years in Liberia, attended the Azusa Street meetings. He heard many African dialects spoken with which he was familiar. A colored sister spoke at length in tongues as the Spirit was pleased to use her. Immediately after she had spoken Brother Mead arose and interpreted the message and gave the name of the tribe in Africa that spoke the language.

It was soon noised abroad that God was giving gracious visitations in Los Angeles, and many workers came from different parts of the country, received the Pentecostal endowment, and returned to their home towns. They became witnesses to what they had actually seen and heard. This resulted in hungry souls tarrying before the Lord until they received "like precious faith," and so the fire spread rapidly. Before the year 1906 closed, the Pentecostal power had fallen on people in many towns and cities on the western coast.

Many preachers were living in and around Los Angeles when the fire struck at Azusa Street Mission. These were the earliest to receive. Many of them became famous workers in the Lord's vineyard. Among the more famous who labored abundantly for the Lord in home and foreign fields were Brother and Sister A. G. Garr, Brother Glenn A. Cook, Sister Florence Crawford, Brother A. H. Post, Brother and Sister Downey, and many, many others. Brother Garr was one of the first to receive the baptism in the Holy Spirit at the Azusa Street Mission. He and Sister Garr felt called to India and went out by faith fully trusting the Lord. They thought they could exercise the faith necessary to receive from the Lord the languages of India, but they found that they needed an interpreter. After having some ministry in India, they went to China. They settled in Hong Kong, where they established themselves in a strong mission station, to and from which hundreds of missionaries came and went, and a great revival of Pentecost sprang up which has never faded out, despite the ravages of war, pestilence and famine. Brother Cook went east and south in the early days of this movement, and hundreds received the Pentecostal baptism under his ministry. He is one of those who worked in the mission and on *The Apostolic Faith*—the first Pentecostal paper published in America.[1] He is still on board, and happy in the Lord at the ripe old age of 79 years. Sister Crawford with Brother Will Trotter established a great work in Portland, Oregon. These have gone on to their reward, but their work still remains, and thousands will rise up in judgment and call them blessed. Brother A. H. Post and Brother Downey were both called to missionary work and were used in the salvation, healing, and baptism of thousands.

It is forty years at this time of writing since the greatest revival of modern times struck at Azusa Street Mission. Forty is a significant scriptural number, and many are expecting a great outpouring of the Spirit in more than Pentecostal effusion. The great revival of Joel has never yet been fulfilled, when the whole solar and physical system will be revolutionized—frightful scenes in heaven above and earth beneath: "blood, and fire, and vapour of smoke: the sun shall be turned into darkness, and the moon into blood, before that great and notable day of the Lord come: and it shall come to pass, that whosoever shall call on the name of the Lord shall be saved" (Acts 2:19-21). So palpable is this coming downpour of the Spirit in the Scriptures that those who reject the present revival are writing and speaking of the coming Pentecost. We fear that it will be so completely after the pattern of Pentecost and this modern effusion that the people who have rejected this as not of God will not recognize it until it is too late.

All kinds and classes of people visited Azusa Street Mission in the first few years of its history. They saw an entirely new thing in the form of modern religious units. It did not evolve from some previous denomination as other new religions had done. It had no specified form of doctrinal tenets. The main doctrine believed and adhered to was that the baptism with the Holy Spirit was exactly like that described in Acts 2:4 and enjoyed by the members of the apostolic church during the first two centuries of the Christian era.

So it could be said that this new thing was the opposite of a theoretical setup. The doctrinal setup began to develop and take on concrete scriptural form as the movement grew, but the movement was based entirely on a supernatural experience. Its proponents discarded the speculative and theoretical and sought the practical demonstration of the sovereign Word of God. Divine healing, speaking in other tongues, and interpretation of tongues became the great outstanding characteristics of the movement. These were all according to the pattern of the early Christian church. Even the dead were raised, and this can be proved on indubitable authority. The writer has seen four people who were raised from the dead. One girl, who has since grown into womanhood and is now living in Santa Ana, California, was dead for four hours. All animation was suspended, but she was brought back by prayer.

The writer has had this wonderful experience since 1908, and he believes that if a true record were made of the number raised from the dead since Azusa Street revival, it would double the number that the apostles and Jesus raised.

Every manner of known disease has been cured by prayer. Broken limbs have been restored, and various miracles as set forth in the promise of Jesus in Mark 16:17-18 have been performed by believers in the name of Jesus. The only limit is our own inherent unbelief.

ENDNOTE

[1]Apparently Ewart did not realize that a paper called *The Apostolic Faith* was published by Charles F. Parham in Topeka, then Baxter Springs, Kansas, and later Houston, Texas. The first publication was in 1898 in Topeka, three years before the outpouring of the Holy Ghost in the city in 1901. Several papers, including one published at Azusa Street, took the name of this original publication.

CHAPTER SEVEN

Finished Work of Calvary and Jesus Name Baptism

The worldwide revival that struck this country in the beginning of the twentieth century had in a few years produced the most distinctive religious unit in the Protestant world. Because of the unique experience of receiving the baptism in the Holy Spirit with the same identifying sign as that received by the first professors of the Christian faith, which plainly involved new doctrinal tenets, all other churches were unfriendly to it. Most of them were violent in their opposition. It was composed of people of almost every faith, including Roman Catholic and Christian Science, baptized by the one Spirit in order to form one body.

The body was formed. A great company had received "like precious faith" in most parts of Christendom. The fire was spreading. Was a new church about to be formed, with distinctive doctrinal tenets? What would it be called? Would it be organized as all other new bodies in the history of Christianity had been?

While people were pondering these questions, God was dealing with a man by the name of William H. Durham. He was pastor of the North Avenue Mission in Chicago, which the Pentecostal experience had already visited. Durham was a man of great earnestness and intense convictions. However, after fighting the new theology for a time, he succumbed to the great desire to receive the identical experience described in Acts 2:4, on which the church was formed. He came out to Los Angeles, went to the Azusa Street Mission, and after tarrying for many weeks finally received the baptism in the Holy Spirit. He received an overwhelming experience. He spoke in other languages with marvelous fluency and received the gift of interpretation. Pastor Seymour, who had already retired after a heavy day, was awakened by the Spirit. He said that the Lord showed him that Brother Durham was to receive the experience that night, so he re-dressed and came downstairs. When he beheld the wondrous sight of the Chicago pastor filled with the Spirit and speaking in other tongues, the power of prophecy descended upon him, and raising his hands over Brother Durham, he prophesied that wherever this man would preach the power of God would fall on the people.

Durham went back to his little church, and instantly the meetings took on new power and impetus. Meetings were held every night of the week, and hundreds flocked there and received "like precious faith" and were satisfied. Writing of those early days in North Avenue Mission,

Pastor Durham stated: "People began to come in considerable numbers. Soon our little place would not hold them. Best of all, God met those who came. We had meetings that ran on through the night and most of them half the night. It was impossible to close them. The teaching was simple: to repent of every known sin, yield fully to God, resting entirely on the finished work of Christ, fully trusting in the precious blood, and then God would pour His Spirit upon them. One after another God met the seekers. It was nothing unusual to hear people at all hours of the night speaking in tongues and singing in the Spirit."

Many notable preachers came to the North Avenue Mission and were filled with the Holy Spirit. These went back to their churches and started to proclaim the new message, and in every case were honored with great and lasting revivals. E. N. Bell, pastor of a Baptist church in Fort Worth, Texas, was one of these. He figured largely in the future, immediate history of this movement. He was the first chairman of the fellowship of Pentecostal ministers known as the General Council of the Assemblies of God. This was in 1914, and Brother Bell held this position again at the time of his death in 1923.

Another who became notably used in this movement and who received the baptism at the North Avenue Mission was A. H. Argue of Winnipeg, Canada. He is still living and has been much used of the Lord for the past thirty years. A great company of Italians received "like precious faith" at Brother Durham's mission, also a crowd of Persian people. These were encouraged to start up among their own people, which they did in the city of Chicago, and so the work spread with great rapidity.

Pastor William H. Durham was intense in his manner of evangelism, and the four walls of the North Avenue Mission could not utilize his talents. When the great preachers of the world would come to Chicago, he would get an interview with them and give them his experience, and like Stephen it could be said of this unassuming preacher, "They were not able to resist the wisdom and the spirit by which he spake" (Acts 6:10). When A. C. Dixon came to Chicago, Brother Durham was granted an interview with him and many other big church preachers. After he had given them his testimony, he was asked what conclusion had this strange experience brought, or what convictions had he arrived at that were different from the rest of Christendom. He promptly answered that "speaking in tongues as the Spirit gave utterance was the infallible evidence of the baptism with the Holy Ghost." Dr. Dixon fairly roared out: "This is utter nonsense, my brother! Don't you see that by making this claim you indict all Christendom?" To this the imperturbable preacher answered: "Sir, they deserve to be indicted."

The *Pentecostal Testimony* was edited and published by Pastor Durham, and was distributed far and wide. It was a journalistic sledgehammer. The articles were provocative. Religious people of all grades were stirred, and the ultimate result was that they either fought themselves out of rank as exponents of the Bible, or else they were convicted and humbled themselves to receive the experience of the baptism. Thousands came to hear Durham preach, and they all went away with the conviction that he was a pulpit prodigy. When he arose, one never knew just what form the sermon would take. One could not take his eyes off the preacher for fear of missing something precious. The longer he talked the more intensely fascinating the Word became. One night he was preaching about our inheritance of apostolic power and quoted Paul's words to the cripple at Lystra: "Stand upright on thy feet" (Acts 14:10). The power of God was mightily upon him, and with blazing eyes and forefinger pointing to a young man who was crippled sitting in the front row, he commanded, "And you stand upright on your feet!" The young man sprang into the air like a kangaroo and ran and leaped and praised God for a perfect healing.

Sometimes a message in tongues would come to confirm the word, and the interpretation would always follow. Sometimes the spirit of rejoicing would fall upon the audience as the preacher would sing a song in another language, in the power of the Spirit. These meetings would be followed by a prolonged altar service where, by the laying on of hands, sick people would be healed and believers filled with the Holy Ghost, speaking in other tongues.

When Brother Durham came into this movement, certain doctrines were being preached in connection with receiving the baptism of the Spirit. The theology was that there were two works of grace, called salvation and sanctification. Then you received the baptism of the Spirit, which was a gift from God. Pastor Durham vigorously opposed the teaching that sanctification was a second, definite, instantaneous work of grace. He said that sanctification was a scriptural experience, but it was gradual, as we advanced in holiness of the truth. We had to grow in grace and in the knowledge of our Lord and Savior, Jesus Christ.

This constituted the first break in doctrinal unity. Those who came out of the Holiness churches were hostile and tried hard to sustain their cherished doctrine. A battle royal was waged throughout the country, but the force of the preached and written Word prevailed, and the movement as a whole accepted the correction as absolutely scriptural. There are still a few die-hards in the movement, but these are inconsequential.

Pastor Durham came back to Los Angeles in 1911. He found all the Pentecostal missions closed against him, but undaunted he gained an entrance to Azusa Street Mission. A great revival instantly sprang up there. The cloud of glory seemed to have lifted from here and floated over to Spring Street, where Brothers Fisher and Studd conducted what was called the Upper Room Mission. Soon the saints began tracking back to Azusa Street Mission, and eventually the two pastors went over to hear Brother Durham preach. Brother Fisher utterly turned the message down, but Brother G. B. Studd said: "That man has a message and he knows he has." Studd eventually left Fisher. Seymour locked the doors of the Azusa Street Mission against Durham, and a large hall on Seventh Street was opened up. Every church and mission emptied into this place until there was hardly standing room, and the glory of old Azusa Street was repeated in the meetings night after night.

Pastor Durham used great wisdom in supplanting the experience called "a second, definite, instantaneous work of grace" with the real experience of sanctification as taught in the Scriptures. He balanced everything up by the Cross of Jesus. He weighed the fictitious experience in that balance and it was found wanting. When he had clearly revealed its inadequate scriptural support, then he fired the second barrel of his gospel gun. It was that God's people must all go deeper. Then he preached real scriptural sanctification. The process was by acceptance, love of, and adoption of the truth, the gradual abandonment to the will of God as revealed by the Spirit through the Word. Here is an experience that is fathomless and lasts throughout the longest life lived in the Spirit.

The writer will never forget his first day in the Seventh Street Mission and, indeed, all the subsequent days. He found it easy to apprehend the message, for he had believed it while still in the Baptist church. He was invited to the platform at the first meeting and took a prominent part as a worker. When Pastor Durham and Brother Van Loon went to hold meetings in Chicago, the writer was selected as overseer of this great and important work. By that time there was very little opposition to the new doctrine, and it was adopted as part of the Pentecostal faith when the movement was first organized in 1914.

Pastor Durham died in Los Angeles in August 1912. The funeral service was held in the Seventh Street Mission. It was filled to capacity. People came from all parts of the Union to be present. A great man had fallen in our Israel, and we all felt our heavy mental and spiritual loss. The funeral sermon was preached by the writer. The text was unique: "And Joseph dreamed a dream, and he told it his brethren: and they hated him yet the more" (Genesis 37:5). We all realized in our sorrow the reality of John Wesley's dying words: "God buries his workers but carries on His work." Few men were the victims of such inveterate animosity among their brethren, and few were more devotedly loved then he. In this he was a partaker of the most crucial sufferings of His Lord and Master.

It would seem that no man is able to handle more than one part of the truth of God, which has ever been associated with reproach and persecution. Pastor Durham knew that his time was short, and many were the earnest exhortations he gave the writer in private regarding his responsibility as his successor in the work in Los Angeles. No pastor was ever harder to follow than he. No one could do things as he did them. No one could imitate him, let alone duplicate him in the pastorate. He seemed to be kept unconscious of the tremendous influence and power he wielded in the new religious world. He would say, with such an intense look in those black, cavernous eyes: "Ewart, pray that I'll keep hidden away in Jesus; for if ever I get the false notion that I'm anything, I'll die so suddenly that you'll wonder what happened."

This was a great doctrinal overhauling in order to get this movement back in full doctrinal fellowship with the apostles of our Lord Jesus Christ, but there were still greater ones to come. Many who survived the first spiritual earthquake miserably failed God in the second and greater one. At the great worldwide camp meeting staged in Los Angeles in 1913, there were hundreds of preachers present from all over the Union and Canada. These brethren had no need to come all the way from their own churches to get in a revival, for they had revivals at their home churches; however, they came. Brothers Scott and Studd provided tents for a great crowd, but they were snowed under with applications weeks before the meeting started.

There was unquestionably a great revival. By a careful count, 364 received the baptism, with the Bible sign of speaking with tongues, within the four weeks of meetings. However, the people were restless, inquisitive, and on the tiptoe of expectancy. Early in the meetings the preachers rebelled against turning the meetings over to Mrs. Woodworth Etter. There was a great desire to hear others of God's servants, who might have a new message that would take us forward to the glory and power of the "faith once delivered to the saints."

One day a preacher spoke from the passage in Jeremiah 31:22. The very suggestion of God's doing a "new thing" struck fire in the minds and hearts of the saints, and from then on to the end of the camp one could hear expressions of the hope that God would soon do a new thing for His people. The new thing was exhibited to those who had ears and eyes to perceive it.

It was the occasion of a baptismal service in the pool near the big tent. Brother Scott had selected Evangelist R. E. McAlister to preach on the subject of water baptism. The preacher preached along in the usual manner, until he came to the division in his sermon of the different methods of baptism versus the scriptural mode. He mentioned the trine immersionist method—baptizing the candidate three times, face downward. He analyzed it thus: "They justify their method by saying that baptism is in the likeness of Christ's death and make a point from the Scripture that Christ bowed His head when He died." Then he continued that the three dips or baptisms were to honor each person in the Godhead—Father, Son, and Holy Ghost. He concluded abruptly by saying "that the scriptural answer to this was that the apostles invariably baptized their converts once in the name of Jesus Christ, that the words Father, Son, and Holy Ghost were never used in Christian baptism."

There was an inaudible shudder that swept the preachers on the platform and the people in the vast arena. The preacher noticed it and stood in awesome silence. Brother Denny, a missionary from China who was sitting down in the front row, mounted the platform in one bound, took the preacher aside, and told him not to preach that doctrine or it would associate the camp with a Dr. Sykes, who so baptized.

Evangelist McAlister resumed his explanation and said that he did not mean to convey the idea that because the apostles baptized in the name of Jesus Christ it was wrong to baptize according to the formula in Matthew 28:19. Thus ended the confusion on the platform, and the audience repaired to the baptismal service, but the gun was fired from that platform which was destined to resound throughout all Christendom, and that within a year. The writer invited Brother McAlister to his home, and he was in close proximity to him for months. On his insistence, Brother McAlister explained his revelation on the name of Jesus: "Lord, Jesus, Christ, being the counterpart of Father, Son, and Holy Ghost, which made Jesus' words in Matthew 28:19 one of those parabolic statements of truth, which was interpreted in Acts 2:38 and other Scriptures." Brother McAlister left for Canada after that, but before he went he deplored anyone causing a split in the movement over this issue.

CHAPTER EIGHT

Baptism in the Name of Jesus Christ

When the camp meeting closed all the pastors went back to their various churches and missions. The writer left Seventh Street Mission and opened up on Main Street, with Evangelists R. E. McAlister and Glenn A. Cook as his helpers. After several months, suitable mission buildings being very hard to get, we decided to accept the invitation of Pastor Elmer K. Fisher and join our people in Victoria Hall on Spring Street. From the very first this union was confirmed by God's blessing. A continuous revival was enjoyed. Many preachers and missionaries sat on the large platform and took part in the ministries. Brother McAlister left and Elder G. T. Haywood from Indianapolis, Indiana, was our special evangelist. Crowds flocked there to enjoy his wonderful Bible teaching. His knowledge of the Word of God was phenomenal.

The writer was the editor of the paper called *The Good Report*. He was supported by the McAlister brothers, who represented the paper on the fields, and it enjoyed a very large circulation. For months God was dealing with the writer about the name of God and its place in the gospel preached by the apostles. When he would obey God and preach on this great and inexhaustible theme, the power of God would fall and people would flock to the altar. We prayed for the sick in the name of Jesus and the results were surprising. Pastor Fisher and Brother A. G. Garr would urge the writer to preach on the wonderful name. However, the restrictions were definitely laid down. We could do many things in the name of Jesus, but were not to do all things in that name. At last the writer decided to obey God and step out with his message, which by this time was clearly defined in his soul. The only way to get apostolic results was to adopt apostolic methods and obey their precepts. If the preaching of Philip, the evangelist, was concerning the "kingdom of God and the name of Jesus Christ," and his way of preaching Christ to the eunuch made that man hungry to be baptized in the name of Jesus Christ, then if we preach the apostolic gospel we will have the same results.

The apostolic commandment is: "And whatsoever ye do in word or deed, do all in the name of the Lord Jesus" (Colossians 3:17). The apostolic anathema is: "Though we, or an angel from heaven, preach any other gospel unto you than that which we have preached unto you, let him be accursed" (Galatians 1:8). The great commission in Matthew 28:19 is the Lord's commandment in parabolic form, and the Spirit gave the revelation of "the name" on the Day of Pentecost.[1] From there on to the end of the apostolic age, the apostolic commandment as above was literally adhered to. If the apostle Peter did not obey Christ's commandment on the Day of Pentecost, then it never has been obeyed. If the words of the Master were to be taken as a formula for Christian baptism, then the Acts of the Apostles presents one of the most colossal contradictions of history. In that case, the church was built on a flagrant act of disobedience. This is confusion worse confounded!

The writer called the pastor and his assistants and told them of his convictions. He told them that he did not purpose to create any trouble for them and would leave quietly and pitch a tent for evangelistic meetings on the east side of the city. Pastor Fisher was very kind and gracious. He said that he appreciated my position and believed that I was sincere, but he could not see my message. He helped me to furnish the tent and gave me his blessing.

The meetings started in the tent on East First Street, just outside Los Angeles, in a town called Belvedere. I preached my first public sermon on Acts 2:38 on April 15, 1914. The message took fire and that night a revival started. Brother Glenn A. Cook had come back from an eastern trip and came out to the meeting that night, accepted the message, and became my assistant in the tent campaign. We purchased a baptismal tank and set it up inside the tent. I baptized Brother Cook and he baptized me, and then the candidates for baptism in the name of Jesus started to flock to the tent.

The tent soon became too small for standing room, and at night we had more on the outside than we had inside. There was a traffic block, and the good church people of Belvedere petitioned the district attorney to order us out; the writer was brought before him on the charge of disturbing the peace. The town constable was a member of the local Baptist church and allowed us to be persecuted by a desperate gang of hoodlums. When we would appeal to him, he would advise us to move our tent further away. He never enforced the law.

These men would bring stink bombs to the meetings, sit in different parts of the tent, set them sizzling under their seats, and then retire. Every devilish device to force us to abandon the meetings was tried. In the end they burned the tent, but we purchased another and continued until we felt that a move was in God's order. The members of the band they called the Owl Gang would follow my wife and me home after late meetings, and after threatening us would peer in at the bedroom windows and try to scare us. However, while our lives were in danger, God was working after the pattern of the old-time apostolic order. All kinds of incurable diseases were healed in the name of Jesus, and people were saved and filled with the Holy Ghost, speaking in other tongues.

One of the greatest, most startling characteristics of that great revival was that the vast majority of the new converts were filled with the Holy Ghost after coming up out of the water. They would leave the tank speaking in other tongues. Many were healed when they were baptized. One woman who was well known in Pentecostal circles used to fight us desperately. She had tracts printed against the message and would come out early on Sundays and stay all day moving around among the people sowing discord, trying to dissuade people from coming there.

One Sunday, according to her own printed testimony, she came out as usual, expecting to continue her fighting tactics. She had just sat down when she heard an audible voice, like thunder in her ears: "If you will ask my servant to baptize you in My name I will heal you." She had been suffering with an inward cancer for years but was afraid to have an operation, and now the doctors said it was too late. She came striding up the aisle just before time to begin the meeting. I met her at the front of the platform. She asked, "Will you baptize me into the name of Jesus Christ after the meeting?" I said, "I certainly will!" When she was baptized her cancer was instantly healed and disappeared, the swelling all subsided, and the women had to cover her with a robe while they pinned up her skirt. She put this experience in a tract, and it has been circulated everywhere.

But God had more surprises in store for us. One night the leader of the Owl Gang surrendered to Christ, informed the gang that he was through with the old life, and exhorted them to get saved. That was the end of our trouble from that quarter. We were in court several times but were not forced to leave. We received an offer to rent a new theater building because the builder was not able to furnish it, and we moved in just across the street. Here the revival continued for months. People visited us from all parts, were convinced, were baptized in Jesus' name and filled with the Holy Spirit in the water after tarrying for years in vain. God had partially transferred the altar to the baptismal font, and the fire would fall on the water.

God took the most spiritual people out of the local Baptist church. Even the superintendent of the Sunday school, Brother E. D. Yeoman, and his wife were saved and filled with the Spirit. In his testimony afterwards he declared that he never was saved until he surrendered to Christ, was baptized in Jesus' name, and received the gift of the Holy Ghost. He is now state chaplain for the Spanish-American War veterans in California.

The church pastor became furious when they lost so many valuable members, and started persecuting us again. One of our preachers prophesied that God would burn down the church if they did not cease fighting. Some months afterward this prophecy was fulfilled. The fire was so fierce and sudden that they never saved any of the costly furniture. The pastor died with sudden sickness.

Missionary Carl Marvin Hensley and wife received the baptism in the Holy Spirit during this revival. The story of his heroism for the name of Jesus Christ in China is well known. We know few missionaries who have suffered more. He was so eager to get back to his beloved Chinese that before the war ended and the high seas were clear of enemy ships and submarines, he secured a way across, partly by airplane and partly by ship. However, the ship he was sailing on was torpedoed by the Japanese, and though the ferocious Japanese tried to kill all on board and leave no trace of the disaster, the lifeboat which Brother Hensley was in escaped their scrutiny. Some on board died during the thirty days they were on the open sea, but he and others landed in India and got back to America safely.

The paper *Meat in Due Season* was wonderfully used of the Lord in spreading Pentecostal truth. People who were too prejudiced to come where the message was being proclaimed would obtain a copy and get convinced. Elder G. T. Haywood, after fighting the new message, was convinced and opened his large mission to Evangelist Glenn A. Cook. A great revival resulted, and from Indianapolis the revival spread throughout Indiana. Brother Cook was mightily used of the Lord in his pioneer revivals in Indiana, Oklahoma, Missouri, and the Southern states. In Indianapolis alone there were 465 baptized into the name of Jesus, and most of these had already received the Holy Ghost baptism or received this experience after being baptized in water according to the Scriptures.

Much bitter hostility was directed against the paper and its editors. However, our motto was to keep sweet and let the other fellow do the fighting. One Eastern writer, who was the editor of a Pentecostal paper, challenged us to prove that the much disputed word *persons* was not used concerning the Godhead. We replied that the only place we could find it is in Job 13:10: "He will surely reprove you, if ye do secretly accept persons." The writer felt the loss of fellowship keenly, but God comforted him.

These papers would be wrapped, addressed, and prayed over by our faithful band of workers. The paper carried conviction wherever it went. Perhaps more were converted to the message through the paper than all our preaching. The very elite of the Pentecostal movement were mightily moved, and a good majority were convinced of the truth. Among these were: Evangelist L. C. Hall, W. E. Booth-Clibborn, E. N. Bell, A. H. Argue, Frank Small, George B. Studd, Elmer K. Fisher, R. J. Scott, G. T. Haywood, W. T. Witherspoon, M. R. Tatman, Delmer White, E. G. Lowe, R. G. Hoekstra, W. L. Stallones, Harry Morse, and many, many others.

The paper revolutionized the foreign field. The message swept through China, Japan, and India, and the missionaries were baptized into the name of Jesus and then preached the message and baptized their converts. In North China this message, through *Meat in Due Season* challenged the missionaries, and most of them accepted it. In Ta Tung Fu, Shansi, North China, Missionary Ramsay accepted the message, and one of the mightiest revivals in modern times swept through the land. Six hundred heathen Chinese were convicted, repented, and were baptized in Jesus' name, most of them receiving the gift of the Holy Ghost with speaking in tongues while yet in the water. Missionaries came from all over North China to see the wondrous sight. In Japan, Missionary Leonard W. Coote accepted the message and God split the sky over their heads and gave them hundreds of souls. In Egypt, Africa, and South America, revivals also broke out in confirmation of the message.

In 1916, the General Council of the Assemblies of God rejected the message of the oneness of the Godhead and baptism into the name of the Lord Jesus Christ. This action forced a sad and serious walkout. By this time the paper, *Meat in Due Season*, was being eagerly read everywhere. The issue was clearly drawn. All the actual Christian baptisms according to the Word of God were performed in or into the name of the Lord Jesus, Jesus Christ, or Lord Jesus Christ, Jesus being the Greek equivalent of the Hebrew *Yahoshua*, meaning "the Lord who saves you." In every formula mentioned as being used in the New Testament records, the name Jesus is the essence. The titles Christ and Lord are attached or added according to the judgment of the official or the evangelist Luke in making the record. There is no mention made in any other Gospel record but Matthew, or in the Acts of the Apostles, of the formula in the words, "In the name of the Father, and of the Son, and of the Holy Ghost."

Some have dared to assert, in the face of this overwhelming witness of many infallible proofs, that the name of Jesus was not used in Christian baptism but the exact formula of Matthew 28:19 was used in every case. However, there are not many who will deny Dr. Faulkner's statement: "There is not a doubt that all the baptisms performed in the early church were performed in the name of Jesus Christ, but that does not prove that Matthew 28:19 should not be in the Bible." Many of the ablest ministers, while still sticking to their belief in the trinity, believe that baptism should be administered in or into the name of Jesus.

In the year 1915, while Pastor E. N. Bell was general superintendent of the Assemblies of God, according to his own testimony, as he was in prayer before starting on an evangelistic and teaching trip, God spoke to him about being baptized into the name of Jesus. The conviction was so irresistible that he called for Evangelist L. V. Roberts, a Oneness believer, to baptize him. He and Brother Rodgers were baptized, and others among the leading trinitarian brethren followed their lead. Brother Bell met with a withering storm of opposition from his brethren, but Brother Bell stood his ground and defended his new position so unanswerably that many, many people were in doubt as to where this would lead. His article in defense of his action was so forceful and convicting that it has been published and republished. It was published in *The Weekly Evangel* of August 1915 in a mutilated form. We do not want to say, for the very good reason that we do not know why Brother Bell, after witnessing a good confession before the world for a short time, changed his mind concerning this great truth. The writer, as editor of *Meat in Due Season*, wrote Brother Bell for his testimony but received a mysterious and evasive reply, asking that I please refrain from writing anything about his case until I heard from him again.

Elder G. T. Haywood received the message and baptized all his people, and was greatly used by God until his untimely departure in proclaiming the name and absolute deity of our Lord Jesus Christ. Through his wonderful expositions the colored people everywhere responded, and very few of the really great leaders among the colored brethren are left in the old ranks now.

Early in the battle over the truth at a campaign in old Seventh Street Mission, where the writer went after he left Belvedere, Brother Bartleman and Brother George B. Studd were baptized into the name of Jesus. Both their testimonies were published in *Meat in Due Season*. I considered it one of the greatest honors God ever bestowed upon me to baptize my brother, George B. Studd, and have him as my assistant in the work at Belvedere Tabernacle for over eight years. Many of the saints and preachers would not believe that Brother Studd had his baptism until after he was baptized in Jesus' name; then he spoke with tongues more than all.

It was in Seventh Street Mission that Evangelist Albert F. Varnell was convinced and was baptized into the Name. He became a useful worker, and many of the missions in the northern part of this state originated in his tent revivals.

Another marvelous victory was the conviction and baptism of Sergeant J. D. Cornwall of the city police force. He was "my Jonathan."

ENDNOTE

[1]Ewart and other Pentecostals often used the word *revelation* to mean the illumination of the Scriptures by the Holy Ghost. Here, since Ewart argued that Peter's command to be baptized in the name of Jesus fulfills Matthew 28:19, it is erroneous to suppose Ewart meant that Peter received a "new" revelation. At most, Ewart believed that the Spirit gave Peter the understanding of using the name of Jesus in baptism while he was preaching, but it is more probable that his words mean that the Spirit through Peter revealed to the people and to us the correct application of Christ's command in Matthew 28:19. We should note that Ewart's argument is based not upon "revelation" but upon logic and reasoning from Scripture.

CHAPTER NINE

The Power of the Name

When the apparent discrepancy became evident between Matthew 28:19 on the one hand and Acts 2:38 with many other verses of Scripture on the other, many ingenious attempts were made to bridge the gulf. Many of the lesser lights came out with the bland statement that the apostle Peter made a mistake and so the issue is between Peter and Jesus. If it were a choice between following Peter or Jesus, every devout soul would know what to do. But the Master stamped the apostles with His own authority. Moreover, if you take that stand you must put Jesus in disharmony with all the apostles including Paul, for they all baptized in the name of the Lord Jesus. So infinitely important did the apostle Paul consider baptism in the name of Jesus that at Ephesus he gave instructions to people who were already baptized to be baptized over again in the apostolic manner. "When they heard this, they were baptized in the name of the Lord Jesus" (Acts 19:5). Philip's theme was, "The kingdom of God, and the name of Jesus Christ," and he, like the apostles, baptized his converts in the name of the Lord Jesus. (See Acts 8:12, 16.)

In an effort to bridge the gulf between the divided factions, many ingenious compromise formulas for baptism were suggested, such as: "To the glory of the Father, Son, and Holy Ghost, I baptize you in the name of Jesus Christ"; "On the authority of Jesus, I baptize you in the name of the Father, and of the Son, and of the Holy Ghost"; and "In the name of the Father, and of the Son, and of the Holy Ghost—the Lord Jesus Christ." All of these baptismal formulas utterly failed, and two of those quoted above were invented by preachers who came out and publicly confessed they were wrong and rebaptized their converts over again in the name of the Lord Jesus Christ.

One of those who accepted the message and was mightily used of the Lord in its propagation was the missionary evangelist Andrew D. Urshan. When he returned from Persia and saw the disunited condition of the Pentecostal movement, he felt very sad. He decided to use his influence to bring the two factions back into unity. However, after much fruitless effort and months of hard work, he came out and confessed his belief in the new message in its entirety. Throughout the years he has stood unequivocally for the absolute deity of Jesus and baptism in His name.

Evangelist L. C. Hall was another great man whom God was pleased to use in the propagation of the apostolic gospel. Evangelist Hall's natural genius was recognized by all who knew him. He seemed too big for this movement; however, his innate humility made him great. The writer was intimately associated with him for over twenty years in the work of the Lord. The love between us never abated, and it was reciprocal. When an old man, weary in body, he accepted the oversight of the Layne Memorial Hall in Pasadena, which was a trinitarian institution, but Brother Hall never changed his beliefs. He used to go off on long evangelistic tours and usually go among the Oneness people, who were always glad to have him preach for them. His great singing soul poured itself out in some of the most spiritual songs we have. His songs when sung in the Spirit would never fail to woo the Holy Ghost down on the meeting.

Evangelist Frank Small of Winnipeg, Canada, was used to put the new message across in a remarkable way. Brother Small assumed the pastorate of the Oneness work in Winnipeg, and for many years had crowds flock to his meetings that were hard to accommodate. They would go from one building to another in search of a building spacious enough. At last they rented the Winnipeg Theatre, and I am told that people would be seen running from the cars at an early hour to get a seat before the seats were all taken. All kinds of startling and almost unbelievable miracles were performed by faith and the laying on of hands, in the name of Jesus. We published the reports of these meetings in *Meat in Due Season*. A continual old-time apostolic faith revival swept the city of Winnipeg and continued unabated for years. Pastor Small's method was not to argue about baptism in Jesus' name but to go ahead and baptize them in the apostolic manner, and God marvelously confirmed this policy.

The writer will never forget the heavenly thrill that swept through his being when after a wonderful meeting Brother George B. Studd came to him and asked him for baptism in the name of Jesus. I always had a deep reverence in my soul for this great man of God. I remember how I bowed my head reverently and said, "Brother Studd, I feel greatly honored." That night in the meeting, Brother Studd told that while we were singing the song "Trust and obey, for there's no other way to be happy in Jesus, but to trust and obey!" that the Lord said to him, "If that obedience and humility is in your heart, you will be baptized today."

When this became known, people were tremendously moved. It was a great testimony for the power of the truth we were proclaiming. Brother Studd never did things half-heartedly. He threw his weight of character, talent, and influence behind the message, new crowds started to attend, and new power and glory swept through the meetings.

In 1918 the writer came down from the North in the days of the influenza plague. A dark pall was spread over the land. He had left Los Angeles thinking that his work was through in that place. In Portland, the saints had secured our consent to pastor the Oneness work, and they bought a lot and were planning to erect a church building. One night I had a vision of a man whom I recognized as M. B. Froseth, the carpenter. He had a blueprint in his hand, and I asked him what that meant. He replied that it was the blueprint of a tabernacle that he was going to build for me in Los Angeles. I came out of it in great wonderment of soul. But the Lord never left me in doubt. The voice said, "The vision is of Me. Return to Los Angeles and I will use you there." I never equivocated. I told my precious wife and called a secret meeting of the church board. They were indignant at first, but when I told the story of my vision and the command of the Master, they reluctantly and sorrowfully agreed to release me of all my obligations.

The awful, devastating war had ended by November. The plague had abated, and we had selected the place to build the tabernacle, with the very man I had seen in the vision consenting to do the work. We had only $200.00 when we ordered the first load of lumber, which Brother Froseth had purchased on a time sales contract. I was to raise the money and he would put up the building. Early in 1919 we had our dedication services, and at the first meeting we raised enough money to clear us of debt.

Brother Studd was my assistant pastor, and how the Lord did confirm this appointment! I gave him a free hand in the missionary fund work. We had a special missionary meeting the first Sunday in each month, and he would read his letters direct from the field and make a strong appeal, which I would always confirm. We were able to send more money to our missionaries than any other Pentecostal mission in United States. Often we would have a special need, and over and above the liberal offering a check would be given up in the hundred dollars. We received several at special appeal times for $1000.00. For eight years there was no other offering taken up unless it was a special need. I was supported by tithes and offerings put in an iron box at the entrance. Brother Studd was the most liberal soul I ever met. If the subject of tithing came up, he would say: "My tithe is all that I can possibly spare over and above my living expenses, and myself with it." This was true.

We had the large auditorium filled and held meetings twice a week and three times on Sunday when we did not have special meetings. Members of our audience came from suburban towns over forty miles distant. The baptismal font was patronized every week; sometimes I would baptize over fifty in one service. I kept a record of the number baptized, and when we stopped because of a fear that we were numbering the people and might incite God's displeasure, there were over two thousand names.

It was a common thing to have the majority of the candidates that had not received the baptism in the Holy Spirit receive the experience in the baptismal font. Miracles were continually taking place. At one service I baptized a Spanish woman 105 years old. She was stone blind. She said that the Lord had showed her that He was coming for her soon, and that she must be baptized in His name. When she descended into the font and stood with hands clasped in prayer, the power of God so wrapped us that we were both mightily quickened. The saints close by said that she raised up and stood still in the water about a foot from the bottom. In a few days this old pilgrim was gone to her reward. God put such a premium on being baptized into His name in those days.

It was simply amazing. Literally hundreds were miraculously healed in the water. I have had people refuse to take off their best clothes, the conviction was so strong on them. Many went with their watches on, forgetting everything in their anxiety to obey God. I have had men unstrap or unscrew their peg legs and, with some help, get down into the font for baptism. I baptized one man in a dying condition on a stretcher because he insisted that God showed him his time had come and he wanted to be baptized into the name of Jesus. We buried him the week after this service.

In the year 1928 a book was published by the American Tract Society that was as startling as its name signified: *A Remarkable Biblical Discovery, or The Name of God*. The author was a layman named William Phillips Hall. It at once commanded nationwide recognition. It was reviewed in *The Literary Digest* very favorably, and it was also reviewed and recommended in *The Sunday School Times*. Someone sent me a copy, and I was pleasantly surprised that the "remarkable biblical discovery," was that "the name of the Father, Son, and Holy Ghost, was Jesus or Lord, Jesus Christ." In his prefatory note, the author stated that the book was written largely at the urgent suggestion of his friend, Dr. A. C. Gaebelein. Brother Hall wrote me confidentially afterwards that Dr. Gaebelein said, "Hall, if there is one theme on which the church is woefully ignorant, it is the name of God."

Although a layman, Mr. Hall had been a student and expositor of the English Bible for some thirty years, but after taking up the study set forth in this book, he discovered that a working knowledge of both Hebrew and Greek would be necessary to success. Taking Dr. Gaebelein's advice, Mr. Hall resigned his many official positions, chief of which was president of the American Tract Society. He had not proceeded very far with his studies when he realized that he was bringing into the light a number of facts of a deeply interesting and very surprising nature. These findings he would bring before the attention of the most eminent men in the theological world, and they verified their biblical validity. This corroborative testimony was of special interest in view of the fact that the findings referred to were evidently of long obscured truths, which were of the most religiously important character.

After long years of careful research work, the manuscript of the book was ready for presentation to the best authorities on such subjects. When a number of these were consulted, he submitted the manuscript to the publication department of the American Tract Society.

When the book came out, there was a consensus of qualified judgment of those to whom the manuscript had been submitted. It was all laudatory. The fact that stares the reader in the face when he gets inside the book is that the consensus of modern scholarship has confirmed the author's most revolutionary and startling findings. These confirmations came from various scholars and devout churchmen who stood at the head of their own particular departments. One is quoted from an eminent Hebraist. After reading the manuscript he wrote the author as follows: "You have done the work in genuine Semite style. Any rabbi would appreciate the Old Testament part of your work. It is well done and correctly done too. The argument is convincing and unanswerable."

At a later date the same authority wrote: "Regarding the underlying central thought of the primary apostolic interpretation of the term, 'The Name of God' brought to the light and understanding of man in this study, apparently after some eighteen hundred years of obscurity and incomplete understanding. I would say, this thing is deeper than the translators realized. In fact they failed to grasp it at all. It cannot be made too plain."

After reading the contents of the evidence set forth in Mr. Hall's book, a university man, an eminent scholar, wrote: "I am conscious of the deity of the Lord Jesus Christ being suddenly and finally lifted above the level of theological dispute. It is no longer a debatable question. If there is any God at all who has revealed Himself unto men, and whom men may worship, He is God!" How deep is the significance of Thomas's words: "My Lord and my God!" (John 20:28).

One of the most eminent and universally recognized scholars in the Christian world, after reading the book, wrote: "I have literally been in a state of rapture, both physically and spiritually, ever since, and the climax was reached today on my way home from church in reading your spiritually illuminating Union with God in Christ. . . . Praise God in Christ, from whom this blessing has overflowed my life. Our interview has created a great hunger for further fellowship. It has also raised the question: How can I aid in spreading the great truths so wonderfully revealed to you? There must be some way by which I can pass on this unanswerable array of evidence of the deity of the Lord Jesus Christ to others who are perplexed, as I have been, over this vital fundamental postulate, on which our faith and eternal life depend. Life has never so appealed to me as now. I want to help you proclaim the good tidings, and hasten the dominion of God in Christ throughout the earth."

When I read the book, I wrote to Mr. Hall and gave him my experience and sent excerpts from *Meat in Due Season* to confirm my revelation of substantially the same truth some ten years previous. He wrote me a very gracious letter and asked permission to keep the excerpts and show them to his scholarly friends. He said this is the miracle of the age "that you should get this hidden truth by revelation, which it took me twenty years of research work to discover."

This started a very profitable and pleasing correspondence between us. I found Brother Hall very gracious in his personality and kindly disposed towards the baptism in the Holy Spirit with speaking in other tongues as in the Scripture. He presented me with an autographed copy of his book, which I prize very much and which is before me as I write. This book has made some astounding inroads into established and orthodox theology. One reader, the minister of the First Christian Church in New York City, was rebaptized into the name of Jesus, and started baptizing his converts in this—the apostolic way. Mr. Hall knew of this incident and I asked him if his message to the world would have that effect, why did not he and all those who had confirmed his findings, obey the message?

The power of tradition was never more fully displayed. All the great men who said that the discovery that the words of Matthew 28:19 were never used in Christian baptism in the apostolic church age continued doing a thing that they acknowledged the apostles never did. This is amazing!

If a saint filled with the Spirit of God will read this book with an open heart and in much prayer, he will be forced to make a decision. Some disposition must be made of the book's appeal. He will either settle down in satisfaction with prevailing traditional custom throughout the churches, nominal and Pentecostal, or he will decide to arise and be baptized, calling on the name of the Lord! There seems to be no other alternative! Dr. R. A. Torrey in his famous work, *What the Bible Teaches*, said, "If we had the normal faith and experience on the earth, we would baptize repentant believers in the name of Jesus Christ, then lay hands on them, and they would receive the Holy Spirit baptism." I told him that he was right, and that we had the normal faith in the Pentecostal phenomenon.

CHAPTER TEN

How the Jesus Name Message Came to Canada

By Frank Small

Since it would appear to be the objective of the Pentecostal Assemblies of Canada to wage battle at this time, openly, against the "Jesus Only" people (so-called) in Canada through the columns of its official organ against certain tenets of faith sponsored by the Apostolic Church of Pentecost of Canada, the writer feels the burden and cause of Christ for progressive truth of many years' standing at heart, referring to Canadian soil. It seems proper and consistent under the present growing misunderstanding that there should be a proper setting forth of all the major facts, that those whom it may concern may be in a position to intelligently judge as to who is who and what is what, so far as "New Issue" in Canada is concerned, and to know who is the shoot and who is the offshoot.

The writer makes no apology for his claims to know certain major facts in the movement's history in Canada relative to doctrine and also organization, being in it from its inception in Winnipeg in April 1907 and being the promoter of the first organization under Dominion charter. He is quite familiar with all the truth and the issues pro and con of a progressive character. The writer is therefore in a position to make certain declarations. He also feels that under the present distress of misunderstanding, occasioned by what he terms inconsistencies in the church that should not be named, and having suffered many things in silence, now there should be a proper setting forth of such facts as will aid the uninformed inquirer to a better understanding in view of the present attack.

It is the purpose of the defense to set forth in this epistle some historical facts referring to basic principles of the Pentecostal movement in Canada, including the remote beginning, with the first message on water baptism in the exclusive rite of Jesus' name and its first usage in western Canada, by whom, when, and where, as follows.

"At the eighth annual Pentecostal Convention held in Western Canada in the City of Winnipeg, November 1913, the first message on the exclusive rite of water baptism in Jesus' name was delivered by the guest speaker for that occasion, namely Pastor R. E. McAlister of eastern Canada. In those days it was not considered a breach of ministerial courtesy for a guest speaker to advance some new truth. The movement of those days had just undergone a revolutionary process by a new message called 'The Finished Work of Calvary,' and it was therefore at that time in a receptive attitude to receive further revealed truth should it come. Too, the young movement was still unorganized, which naturally would facilitate any such possibility. However, the guest speaker did not hesitate to deliver his revolutionary message pending a baptismal service. Imagine such a thing as that happening today! All would be consumed and obscured in a dustcloud.

"At any rate, the guest speaker very ably analyzed the New Testament Scriptures, proving very emphatically in every instance that the apostles of Jesus baptized by single immersion in the exclusive rite of Jesus' name. The writer was asked to do the baptizing at the conclusion of the said service. Nothing was said to him as to what formula he should use, since a new one had appeared. Having listened to the oration and knowing the new message was based on the simple Scriptures 'in his name' (although the writer heretofore had not followed this exclusive rite in this new and scriptural way), he took the same liberty in which the new message was delivered and baptized thirty candidates in the name of Jesus Christ. This was the remote beginning of the said 'New Issue' in Canada. No objections were raised by anyone present.

"During the years 1914-1915 by the illumination of Scriptures, the new message had resolved itself into the fullness of God in Christ (II Corinthians 5:19; I Thessalonians 5:18; I Timothy 3:16). This teaching developed in the city of Los Angeles, California.

"It might be stated that up till this time the message on water baptism was merely based on records only, without any illumination as to why the apostles so baptized. But in the fullness of time when further illumination on the Scriptures came, proving the absolute fullness of God in Christ (Colossians 2:9-10), then it was clearly understood why the apostles of Jesus used that exclusive rite. Out of this development of the truth came the action of rebaptizing in this exclusive rite in the city of Los Angeles. Hundreds of thousands were obedient among the ministry and laity, with the result that as early as the latter part of June 1915, this new advance message was sweeping Canada and practically all Christendom."

—Frank Small
Editor, *Living Waters*

CHAPTER ELEVEN

Revival in Canada

By L. C. Hall

Beginning in Toronto, Canada, the 14th of November, and continuing one month, it was our joy, with Elder George A. Chambers of Berlin, Ontario, Canada, to open this campaign in a large vacant church.

Our first audience numbered about a dozen. Before the meetings closed they had increased to six hundred. Having gone through our own invitation we did not ask or expect the cooperation of other missions or workers. The enemy was busy, by pen and voice, warning the people to stay away. "Heretics" and kindred epithets flew through the air and mails. Warnings and entreaties proved futile, for the people wanted to know about the one true God revealed in Jesus Christ our Savior.

Soon the light began to break. God's blessing and power fell upon the message. As many began to see the light, they desired baptism in the only name given under heaven among men, whereby we must be saved. (See Acts 4:12.) There was no baptistry in the church, but hearing of a transportable one gotten up through the ingenious mind of Elder R. E. McAlister of Ottawa, Ontario, we sent for it. It can be folded or put into a trunk. Eighty-four were baptized in His name, including eight or ten preachers. Among them was Elder T. H. Gilbert, in charge of one of the missions in Toronto.

Our meeting was in the neighborhood of three large universities. Many attended from these, and some of the theologians were baptized in His name, afterwards receiving the baptism of the Holy Spirit according to the scriptural pattern. Reports from Toronto since the meeting closed are that God is still blessing and great numbers are obeying and receiving the Holy Ghost.

Our next meeting was at Parry Sound, a beautiful little city on the shores of the Georgian Bay. Elder Alexander was in charge. He, his wife, and about all of his assembly saw the truth and were baptized into the name of the Lord Jesus Christ.

We arrived at Ottawa in time to attend the closing of Brother R. E. McAlister's convention, conducted by Elder G. T. Haywood of Indianapolis, Indiana. He left for Kinburn with Brother Charles E. Baker to hold a convention. We continued the meeting for one week. About 112 were baptized in Ottawa in the only name given, during this great campaign. Brother Haywood was in Kinburn about ten days, and we continued through the week. I believe that fifty-six were baptized in the only name.

Our next meeting was in Berlin, Ontario, with Elder Chambers in his own mission. It had been our privilege to preach at his camp meeting the summer before and to open up that part of Canada to this wonderful message. The message was attended with revival fires. Hundreds obeyed the gospel and were baptized in the name that is above every name. A great number were healed and born into the kingdom of God while in the baptismal waters.

The fight is on, the battle is real, victory is sure in Jesus' name.

—Evangelist L. C. Hall
Reprinted from *Living Waters*

CHAPTER TWELVE

The Great Winnipeg Revival

One of the greatest Pentecostal revivals in modern times was that which God gave Pastor Frank Small in the city of Winnipeg, Manitoba, Canada. The writer was with Pastor Small when he opened up his first mission. The only building that we both could accept was an old Jewish synagogue. The floor was crumbling in, and the entire building needed renovating. When we gained admission, our first impressions were very unfavorable. However, the power of God fell on us simultaneously and witnessed that this old, forsaken building was God's choice. The tent meeting on the Red River outside the city of Winnipeg was yet in full swing. It had been wonderfully owned and confirmed by the Lord, but when Pastor Small entered his new work in the city by opening up that renovated Jewish synagogue, a veritable Pentecostal effusion was poured out and lasted for years without a break.

The writer went back to Los Angeles, California, and month after month the reports of this astounding revival appeared in the paper called *Meat in Due Season*, and the readers of this paper read them with delight and amazement in all parts of Christendom.

It was disclosed that this great revival was a definite answer to earnest prayer which Pastor Small and his faithful few had been engaged in day after day and night after night for months. The avenues of approach to the mission in the synagogue were blocked with crowds, until the doors were closed and hundreds of disappointed people turned away. The most remarkable characteristic of these meetings was that they were more kindred to the revivals described in the Acts of the Apostles than anything else in the religious modern world.

As in the beginning in Los Angeles, God set His signal stamp on baptism in the name of Jesus by healing and baptizing believers in the water. No one without the baptism in the Holy Spirit was expected to leave the baptismal font without receiving the Spirit, and very few did. Incurable diseases that had baffled physicians and the prayers of the saints for years were healed in the act of being baptized into "the name above every other name." When the writer saw people being healed under his hands while being baptized in the name of Jesus when he did not even pray for their healing, he went to the Lord about it, and God showed him that all blessing was centered in the name of God and His Word.

Besides the candidates being healed and filled with the Holy Spirit in the water, all kinds of special miracles were wrought in the name of Jesus. The glory of God would descend upon the pastor and candidate, and they would become lost to themselves. The candidates after being baptized would rise to a level of a foot above the bottom and stand there with uplifted hands and heavenly faces praising God. These things gave a supernatural feature to the Winnipeg revival that signally stamped it as of divine origin and made people confess that God was in the place.

No building obtainable would hold the crowds that flocked to these meetings night after night, week after week, month after month, and year after year. The Winnipeg Theatre was rented, and we were told that people could be seen getting off the streetcars as early as six o'clock in order to obtain a seat for the evening meetings.

Pastor Small adopted the policy of baptizing the candidates into the name of Jesus without telling them why, at first. But he soon discovered that the miracles that happened in the water made people inquire after the power at the back of it all. He would then inform them that it was because they did everything in the name of Jesus, which is the name of the Father, and of the Son, and of the Holy Ghost; the only name given under heaven among men whereby we must be saved; the name that is above every name that is named; the name in which every knee shall bow and every tongue shall confess that Jesus Christ is the Lord of the universe to the glory of God the Father. Amen. Multitudes will rise up on the day of judgment and call Pastor Small blessed!

CHAPTER THIRTEEN

The Great Outpouring in China

In the year 1807 the first missionary, Robert Morrison, arrived in China. In the city of Macao, he and William Milne began their missionary labors for China. It was here that probably the first Protestant Christian convert was baptized and the first Protestant Christian church was organized. It was here again in October 1907, just one hundred years later, that the first Pentecostal missionary landed. The missionaries were gathered for a summer conference. The Lord had prepared many of them for the message. Missionaries connected with many missionary societies were graciously and gloriously baptized in the Holy Spirit, according to Acts 2:4. It is estimated that two hundred Chinese and missionaries were baptized in the Spirit, speaking with other tongues.

Miss Moonmau, a missionary in China, on hearing of

the baptism in the Holy Spirit being poured out in America, left China and went straight to Los Angeles. In October 1906, she sought and received the baptism with signs following.

Of the revival that followed after her return to China, she has this to say:

"A Chinese woman, who was very ill, was taken to the mission hospital and returned home in despair unhealed. A testimony of healing was given to this woman's husband, who had been a member of the denominational church from which he had been expelled because of gross sins. The wife, who was suffering from typhoid fever, was in a critical condition. We dealt with them faithfully on the lines of faith and obedience. God answered prayer, and in a few days this woman was able to walk a distance of about four miles to the mission.

"This healing was the beginning of a wonderful work of grace in this woman's life, also in the lives of her family and near relations. The Holy Ghost wrought mightily in her in convicting power.

"Her husband was soon gloriously saved, confessing his sins and making restitution. He had a relative who was an idol worshiper and who, on hearing his relative's testimony, was saved. This man had a very sick child. The child was anointed with oil in Jesus' name and in a short time began to mend. This child's healing resulted in the conversion of the relatives.

"Numbers of demon-possessed people have been gloriously delivered through the power of Jesus' blood, including some insane people. One of these had been insane for over nine years. So violent was he that he would at times break the chains that bound him. With the consent of the mother of this man, the images were smashed and burned. A message on salvation was given to the crowds of people present. Then the crazy man was prayed for. That night he rested much better than usual. In a few days' time he could help his mother cook. In a few weeks' time he was instantly and completely delivered and returned to the government job he had left. The day he was prayed for, his mother was saved and delivered from opium smoking and gambling, and in a short time she received the infilling of the Holy Spirit, speaking with other tongues.

"In the same house as this lunatic was an epileptic. One day while resting on the couch, she had a seizure. With eyes closed, teeth clenched, pale countenance, and body rigid, in response to an inquiry she suddenly moved her head, indicating that she desired to be prayed for. Besides the workers, a number of Christian neighbors gathered to join in prayer. Outside in the courtyard was a large crowd of people who could plainly see through the windows this afflicted woman and the praying band. The uncle in the courtyard was raging, and he threatened to hang us if the girl died. Inside the house the spirit of prevailing prayer continued for almost an hour. Suddenly the epileptic began to sing in her own native tongue, 'Jesus breaks every fetter,' and in a few moments she sat up, and with arms uplifted continued to sing, 'I will shout hallelujah, for He sets me free.' From that time on she never had another attack. The crowds of neighbors were amazed at the power of the living Christ."

Miss Appleby is well known to the writer, as I was pastor of the Pentecostal church in Winnipeg, Canada, when she and the Dennys first went to China. She has so many marvelous and astounding stories to tell of God's power in those revival days that they alone would fill a book.

In the latter part of 1926, W. W. Simpson wrote from Minchow: "Your labors and prayers and offerings have resulted in a mighty revival and the sending forth of 27 additional laborers into the great harvest field. On June 8, a man came to the meeting from Taochow, asking Mr. Chow, who has charge of the work there, to come and pray for his niece who had been sick about three months and was now dying but wanted to be saved ere she passed away. They hurried to her bedside, and after prayer she was saved; then the two workers prayed for her healing. The next morning they were called again and saw that the woman was dying. According to the Chinese custom she was already dressed in her burial clothes. Her limbs had lost all feeling and were growing cold and stiff. Her father, the doctor, and all her family knew she was dying, but the two men of God held on in faith. Finally she ceased breathing and her tongue dropped back into her throat. But the two men still kept their hands on the life-less body, praising the Lord for victory over death.

"After a few minutes they heard one word from the dead throat—'faith.' Reassured, they redoubled their praises, and soon the mighty Spirit of life from Jesus Christ filled that mortal clay and all heard clearly the dead lips speaking in tongues as He gave utterance! And the same Spirit who gave utterance in tongues raised that dead woman to life. Calling to her father, the Spirit through her said: 'Except you believe in Jesus, your daughter cannot live.' Her father dropped to his knees and accepted the Lord he had rejected for over thirty years. The Spirit through her then told her husband that he, too, would have to accept Jesus as his Lord and Savior. When he said, 'Yes, I will believe,' the Spirit through her said, 'It must be with all your heart,' and he confessed his sins and accepted the Lord. The Spirit through her said, 'There are three who are mocking,' and her husband looked outside and saw three members of an idolatrous family mocking at the Word of God. The Spirit through her challenged them to prove their religion, and the Spirit of God declared through her, 'To show that Jesus is true and your religion false, I will cause this woman to stand on her feet today, sit up tomorrow, and walk on the third day.'

"Immediately with no assistance and to the consternation of all, the woman who was dead just a few moments before stood up in their midst and preached the gospel for two and one-half hours. She, who had never heard the Bible read and could not read a word herself, proclaimed the terrible judgments now impending, going over much the same ground as the Revelation! The next day she sat up, and the third day she walked in the presence of many. As a result of this mighty miracle her entire family has been saved and deep conviction has come to many others. Her father came sixty miles to the Minchow convention to tell about it and to be baptized."

In 1927, a blessed outpouring of the Spirit came to the Baptists in a Chinese church in Canton. Those in charge of the school became alarmed and sent for the head teacher from Shanghai to come down and stop the movement. But she was taken sick and was healed in the Pentecostal mission in Canton and received the baptism with the Holy Ghost, speaking with other tongues. Also another one of her companion teachers received her baptism in the Presbyterian compound, in the school for the blind. A Chinese lady doctor has lately been filled with the Spirit; she has left her hospital work and gone out to preach the gospel. Another remarkable report is regarding an old lady who was miraculously saved and whom God has used to bring hundreds into the kingdom. She is over eighty years of age. Lately God has given her a wonderful faith in praying for the sick. Hundreds are now coming to her for prayer, and a great revival has broken out. Some twenty-five received the baptism under her ministry in two weeks' time.

However, as great and wonderful as all other revivals in China have been, none excel the mighty awakening that came to the Ka Do tribe under the ministries of Brother and Sister Baker. Brother Baker and his wife gathered together in the city of Yunnan a number of children. Brother Baker writes: "There was a very remarkable revival of the Spirit among the Chinese children of the Adullam mission in Yunnanfu, China. The children, mostly boys, the majority below the teen age, had nearly all been rescued from a beggar's life on the streets of the city.

"Meetings were held with these children twice a day. Suddenly in one of these services the heaven opened, and the veil was so drawn aside that these children were allowed to see the invisible things of the other world as face to face. This continued for a period of eight weeks.

"The first two weeks the glory of God rested upon the place so that all ordinary activities were suspended, while the things of the Lord were sought earnestly day and night. Sleeping or eating seemed but mere incidents.

After going to bed, children would often get up again and return to the prayer room to seek the Holy Spirit and be lost in heaven-sent blessings until morning. Almost all the time, day and night, there were those who lay prostrate under the power of the Lord, lost in the things beyond the veil. At times the glory of the New Jerusalem seemed to descend upon the group, who were in vision dancing with the angels, though in reality they were dancing in the prayer room, sometimes describing in prophecy what they were seeing in vision.

"Walking through the streets of the New Jerusalem in vision, visiting mansions of indescribable glory, playing by the streams of the heavenly Eden. Enjoying the delicious fruits, flowers, and birds and other glorious wonders of paradise more than restored, and ten thousand wonders that cannot be told. These children seemed to be translated from earth to heaven. They thought that they actually left their bodies and ascended through the first heaven, where they could feel the heavenly air as a breeze on their faces. Then on through the starry realm and on through the third heaven into the golden city.

"By anointing children as well as older ones and sending them out to preach in the power of God, the Lord seemed to be showing what He wants the final church to be in the last days of its testimony upon the earth.

"A new door was miraculously opened by God. A young married man of the Ka Do tribe who had never heard the gospel, but who knew a little about the claims of Christianity to present a way of getting through this present life without the heavy demands of constant sacrifices to appease the devils, for material motives more than any other decided to become a Christian.

Accordingly he discussed this with the other fifteen families of his village.

"This village was soon followed by other villages turning to Christianity in a mass movement until there were six hundred families. At this time I was invited to be the first missionary to visit the movement. I found God had prepared hearts everywhere and these heard the gospel for the first time in their lives. This mass movement soon spread to ten thousand people.

"The young man who had first decided to become a Christian returned with us to the Adullam Mission on the first trip into Ka Do land. He was converted and received the Holy Spirit, and after a few weeks he returned to his home in the mountains. He was uneducated and knew only the fundamental things of the Lord. But upon his return to his village and his telling his people about the Holy Spirit falling among the children at our home, where he had received the Holy Spirit baptism, the people in the village wanted to seek the Holy Spirit.

"This they did, and He fell upon them mightily. This fire of God spread rapidly to other villages. Other young men now came with the former one to the Adullam Mission in Yunnanfu to learn more of the Lord, study the Bible, and seek the Holy Spirit. Their stay was short, but as soon as they arrived the Holy Spirit began to fall among them in mighty power, until all who came received, some speaking in other tongues and prophesying. The importance of leading men and women to Christ was always emphasized to them in the meetings.

"Upon their return to their native homes in the mountains, they went everywhere among the villages preaching repentance, the soon coming of the Lord, and the need to receive the power of the Holy Spirit, and to give a real testimony in the midst of a wicked generation. Everywhere these men went, the Lord poured out the Holy Spirit. Within a few months the fire spread all over Ka Do land and into the other tribes, until the villages where no one had received the Holy Spirit were very few."

Brother Baker has written so many articles and books about this revival among the Ka Do people that the story is well known in America. However the revival goes on without any appreciable letup. The people themselves are the preaching power that God uses. It is estimated that some three thousand of these Ka Do people have been won to Christ.

For the forty years since the great worldwide awakening at Azusa Street, Los Angeles, California, the Pentecostal phenomenon has been reaching out to all parts of the earth.

It would be most invidious to close this chapter on the missionaries who wrought so nobly in the great missionary fields of China without mentioning the veteran missionaries Reverend and Mrs. D. K. Sheets. Sister Sheets went out to China among our earliest Pentecostal workers, and her love for the people and unflagging zeal and consecration enabled her to cover a period on the field of over thirty years. She went out years before she was married to our Brother Sheets. They have two books to their credit about their missionary work in China, and no one can read them without being profoundly moved with gratitude to Almighty God that He was able to inspire such devotion and sacrifice for His people and His kingdom in two human hearts.

These two efficient and noble missionaries are again back at their stations in the Orient. The missionary work has been made more hazardous and much more difficult than in the years before the war. China has perhaps suffered more from the ravages of continuous war than any other nation on earth, and the end has not yet come, as civil war, savage and unrelenting, has sprung up among her people.

There is no class of people that suffers both directly and indirectly because of the ravages of war more than the missionaries do. Yet they bravely fight on, looking for their reward to the city whose builder and maker is God. Amen.

Space forbids telling of the noble work of so many other, both ancient and modern, missionaries who have done commendable work in the missionary fields of the Orient. Missionary Ramsey and his band of noble, self-sacrificing missionaries deserve most honorable mention. They were the first to herald the apostolic gospel in the great province of Shansi, and stuck year after year, praying and toiling until God rewarded their efforts with one of the most marvelous revivals of modern times. (This revival is referred to in another chapter in this book.) In this revival the pure, apostolic gospel on the blueprint of Acts 2:4 and Acts 2:38 was so proclaimed that God's confirmation of the same was the nearest thing to that recorded in the Acts of the Apostles we have ever contacted in modern times. Within six weeks, six hundred heathen Chinese repented of their sins, were baptized into the name of Jesus Christ, and received the Holy Spirit baptism with the sign following. Sister Elizabeth Stieglitz, who is now waiting for her shipping reservation to return to China, had a vital part in this great revival. So many more are deserving of honorable mention in these pages, but our space forbids. God will reward them all, and that beyond their most sanguine expectations.

Missionary Coote and workers had done a real, worthwhile work in Japan before all missionaries were ordered home because of the war. Thousands of Japanese have been brought into the Pentecostal experience through their untiring missionary devotion. Brother Coote had a large compound for years in Japan and trained the workers who were called of God, both natives and those from the homelands.

Shortly after the Japanese armies had brought Manchuria under their control, the Christian churches of Japan became stirred with compassion for the Chinese people. They decided to send missionaries to this great field, and one of the pastors came to Mukden. He was a very active man and in a short time had a good, wholesome gospel work under way. The support of these missionaries was undertaken by the missionary-minded Christian churches in Japan.

CHAPTER FOURTEEN

The Gospel Invades India

In keeping with the history of all great revivals, the outpouring of the Spirit in India was preceded with long, heart-searching seasons of prayer. As in most of the phenomenal interventions of God in answer to the prayers of the saints, the revival was centered around one person in the beginning. God invariably starts by honoring a man or woman with a vision. Pandita Ramaba, a native Christian, was the one God used.

She keenly felt the need of a revival in her work at Mukti and called for volunteers among her girls to pray it down. Some seventy sincere girls volunteered, and prayer was made to God without ceasing. By the time God answered with a mighty deluge of the latter rain, there were over five hundred people meeting twice daily.

The fire enwrapped one of these volunteer missionary

girls who had responded to Ramabai's call to leave her secular duties and go forth to the villages around Mukti to preach the gospel. The amazing story runs: The young woman sleeping next to her awoke suddenly, and seeing the fire enveloping her, screamed for help, jumped out of bed, ran across the dormitory, brought a pail of water and was about to dash it upon her where she still lay in bed, when she discovered that the girl was not on fire. It was a vastly different kind of fire. When this innovation became known, most of the young women in the compound gathered around. They wept and prayed, confessing their sins, as the prophet Isaiah did when he saw the vision of the Lord. Then the newly fire-baptized saint stood up, told what God had done for her, and exhorted them to repentance.

The next evening, while Ramabai was expounding the Scriptures, the Holy Spirit fell on the class and all the girls broke out praying aloud. God was dealing with them, and they could listen to no one else. From that day the two assembly rooms were turned into a kind of modern inquiry room. Regular Bible lessons were suspended, and the Holy Spirit gave the leaders a real, supernatural ministry. This was not based on what they knew, or on the result of their studies in the Scripture, but startling messages on repentance, confession, and assurances of salvation based on the grace of God alone. This would bring solid, scriptural conviction for sin and a resolute determination to forsake it, and the result would be a real infilling of the Holy Spirit with speaking in tongues and other manifestations of the Spirit. When once the real, scriptural sample of the wonderful experience was put on exhibition, then the others would accept nothing short of that. When they got it, they would cry: "I got it!" and "This is that!"

The joy of real possession was so overwhelming that it provided the recipients with utter satisfaction, and they would sometimes go for days at a time without eating any food.

The fire spread rapidly, and a great number were continuously being added to the company of believers by the baptism with the Holy Spirit. Thus a church or body of believers was formed after the apostolic pattern, for in one Spirit were they all baptized to form one body. (See I Corinthians 12:13.) The good tidings spread far and wide. At Dhond, Albert Norton, the beloved missionary, came to Mukti Mission, to see and hear for himself. His own words are: "About six months ago we began to hear of Christian believers in places over a widespread area, receiving this experience of the baptism with the Holy Ghost and fire, speaking in languages that they had never known before. I went to the mission on invitation of Sister Abrams. She took me into a room where a score of girls were praying. After entering I knelt with closed eyes by a table a little removed from the company of seekers. I was startled to hear some of these girls praying to God in English. I was struck with astonishment, as I very well knew that there was no one in this mission who could speak English but Sister Abrams.

"When I opened my eyes I was surprised to see a woman whom I had baptized in 1899 and whom I had known as a devoted Christian worker. Her native tongue was Marathi, and she could also speak a little Hindustani, but she neither spoke nor understood English—the English she was using. When I heard this woman speaking English, distinctly and fluently, well, I felt just as I would have felt had I seen one whom I knew to be dead raised back to life again. Many other girls were speaking in good English, but some were speaking other languages which I didn't understand.

"Why God should permit these young girls to speak in English and not in any of the known dialects of India or some other language unknown to them, I cannot understand. But I have an idea that it is in mercy to us poor missionaries from Europe and America, who, as a class, seem to be harder to convince than any other. All such doubting Thomases in regard to the real scriptural baptism, described in the Scriptures, are not enjoying the power of the Holy Ghost in our ministry as is our privilege."

Brother Norton tells a very touching story, which we feel impressed to record here for the saints' edification: "I was very much impressed with the speaking of a Hindu woman who was rescued in the famine of 1897. She was praying in English. Among other things, she was saying: 'Oh, the love! the love! the love of Jesus! Oh, my precious Lord! My precious Lord! My precious child!' One not knowing her history could not understand the force of the last sentence. The child she mentioned was an only child from whom she had been separated for ten years and with whom she is not allowed to have communication. I was struck with the English which she used, the words being a grade she would not have used had she been learning by study. I have no doubt from what I have known of her that she, by her own powers, could no more have spoken English than she could have taken wings and flown away."

To preserve for our posterity a record of the marvelous character of this Indian Pentecostal outpouring, we have selected the following incidents from different records: Miss Minnie Abrams tells of a meeting held by one of the Mukti bands in Anrangabad in 1906. It was in the Church Missionary Society schoolroom. A little girl of nine was wonderfully anointed with prayer. Before going back to the Church Missionary Society boarding school in Bombay, from which she had come for a vacation, she asked her father if anyone might receive the Holy Spirit. He told her that God would give the Holy Spirit to all who asked Him.

On returning to the school she succeeded in getting four girls to join her in prayer, daily, for the Holy Spirit. Upon one of these, a girl of sixteen, the Holy Spirit was poured out with speaking in tongues. She asked daily to retire to a room for prayer. She would become oblivious to her surroundings and time, wholly occupied in communion with God, praying always aloud. When it was discovered that she was speaking in a language not understood, Canon Haywood was brought in. He decided that this might be the speaking in tongues and took measures to find out what she was saying. In the cosmopolitan city of Bombay, where many languages were spoken, he found one who could understand much of what she said. She was pleading with God for Libya in North Africa. She did not always speak in the same language.

Miss Abrams tells the following incident that took place in Mukti early in 1907: "At midnight, from a room where three head matrons were sleeping, an English hymn rang out in a clear voice, followed by prayer. Manoramabai (Ramabai's daughter) sent word to me that Gulabbai was praying in good English. That night no one went near her to disturb her. At the close of the Sunday school service, she felt she must pray. She asked Miss Carrie Couch to join her in prayer. In a few minutes, Gulabbai was lost to her surroundings and was praying in English. Miss Couch sent for Pandita Ramabai, her daughter, myself, and one by one for all the English-speaking people in the place. All had known Gulabbai since the time she had driven over the mountains, a sad, oppressed Brahmin widow, unable to read a word of any language, unable to speak anything but Marathi. We knew she did not understand English.

"That day tongues became a sign, not to those who believed, but to the Mukti workers who believed not. For four hours she prayed continually. She seemed to crave fellowship in prayer, and in our ignorance we prayed in English, thinking she would understand. At last someone prayed in Marathi. Immediately there was a response, and after a season of prayer in Marathi, the burden of prayer was lifted and the prayer service closed. Gulabbai prayed in Sanskrit the following Sunday morning in the church. Ramabai and Mr. D. G. B. Godre both testified that she used perfect, classical Sanskrit while under the power of the Spirit. She has since spoken Guzerathi and Canarese, all of which languages are unknown to her.

"The power of the Holy Spirit that rested upon Gulabbai was marked. Others began to speak in unknown tongues. The effect was wonderful. Unsaved ones, hitherto unreached, began to seek the Lord. The discouraged ones were encouraged, and those who felt that they could not live a victorious life, repented of their sins. Daily the number of those who spoke in tongues increased."

The well-known journalist, William T. Ellis, was visiting India in 1907. He wrote a lengthy article in the *Chicago Daily News* concerning what he saw in Mukti. He was amazed at what he saw in this revival. He spoke to Ramabai concerning this, and he states that she said to him: "We do not make a special point of the gift of tongues, but our emphasis is always put upon the lives. Undoubtedly the lives of our girls have been changed. About seven hundred of them have come into the place. We do not exalt the girls who have been gifted with tongues, nor do we in any wise call special attention to them. I move among the girls listening to them in awe and wonder. I have heard girls who knew no English at all utter prayers in your tongue. I have heard others pray in Greek and Hebrew and Sanskrit, and others in languages that none of us understood. One of my girls was praying in this very room a few nights ago. She prayed so clearly and beautifully in English."

Miss Sarah Coxe tells how the Spirit of God was poured out on the station of the Christian Missionary Alliance at Gujarat: "We were a most needy lot of missionaries, and our Indian people also needed a new touch from God. We had heard that God was working in America and other parts of the world, and so we began to wait upon Him. From the very first our waiting times were seasons of blessing. God kept searching our hearts and cleansing us, and getting us ready for the great gift He was about to give us, even the baptism in the Spirit. One of our Indian evangelists received a mighty baptism. One day he came to our station at Kaira, where we were all on our faces seeking God. I shall never forget the shine on his face. To look at him just made one desperately hungry for God. He spent most of his time in prayer, and when he gave a message, it was in the power of the Spirit.

"One day he came into the bungalow and said he had been walking and talking with God all around our compound, and that God had told him He was soon going to pour out His Spirit upon Kaira. It was soon after this that the Spirit of God fell upon our missionaries and school (we had then about four hundred Indian girls), carrying everything before Him in a mighty Pentecostal revival. Our Indian Christian girls would gather in groups to pray, some in the schoolroom, some in the veranda, others under a tree, and the missionaries in the bungalow. A mighty wave of prayer ascended to God like an incense. It reached His throne, touched His heart, and He came down and met us. Sometimes these prayer meetings lasted all night.

"One after another we missionaries and our Indian Christians were baptized according to Acts 2:4. One little Indian girl was so happy that she had been baptized that she laughed and laughed and finally went up to Mrs. Shoonmaker, who lived with us, and said, 'God loves me as well as He does you. I am black you are white, but He has given me the baptism, too.'

"Later on that same morning I went out to meet the fifteen girls. They said, 'Why have you not received the baptism when God is pouring down the rain? Shall we pray now?' I said, 'Yes,' and they began to pray. In a few minutes all fifteen were pleading with God for me, and soon I began to pray under the power of the Spirit, then fell back on the floor. It was very hot on the cement floor in India. That very day I was really and truly baptized in the Spirit according to Acts 2:4. I received the baptism of the Holy Spirit and spoke in tongues as an evidence of the baptism. The little girls ran to tell Mrs. Shoonmaker. They asked, 'Did you know that Miss Coxe is in the Pentecostal boat, too?'"

In January 1907, A. G. Garr and wife came to Calcutta, where a number of missionaries were assembled in a convention. These two missionaries had come from the big Los Angeles revival centering at Azusa Street Mission. Brother Garr was one of the very first white men to receive his baptism. God marvelously used them in this convention, and a large number of workers received the baptism according to Acts 2:4 and went to their various stations to teach and preach the glad tidings.

Water H. Clifford, a missionary who was laboring in North India, paid a visit to Ceylon and held some meetings in a number of churches in Colombo and other cities. The Lord confirmed His Word with the signs following. People were healed of tuberculosis, blindness, and deafness. The dumb spoke, the lame walked, and literally hundreds sought the Lord and were saved.

Brother Clifford writes: "In the spring of 1924, while on our way home on furlough, we stopped off in Ceylon and held meetings. Again the Lord blessed." In 1925, Brother Clifford settled permanently in Ceylon. In the first three years, he reports that he had records of over two thousand people coming to the altar for salvation. The revival spread so rapidly that one of the missionaries said, "I would place the number of Pentecostal people in the Island today at over fifteen hundred. Hundreds who have never received the baptism in the Holy Spirit have been healed and saved."

Missionary Maynard Ketcham, in an address given in 1938, said, "It is a joy to report that at the present time the Pentecostal message is making remarkable advance in denominational circles. Several missionaries, some of them holding key positions in their respective missions, have recently received the baptism in the Holy Spirit. Others are earnestly seeking.

"I have personally had the privilege of being associated with a work that is being maintained by Abdul Munshie, a dear Indian brother who is working as a faith missionary in East India. This brother was saved as a boy. His open confession of Christ so enraged his Mohammedan parents that more than once they attempted to take his life. He received the baptism in the Holy Spirit and was called to take up his abode in the ancestral home in East Bengal—cut off entirely from all visible means of support—to live in the midst of a hotbed of fiery opposition. Many meals were provided by God in answer to prayer.

"The marvelous ministry of healing the sick given to this brother was largely instrumental in breaking down prejudice and winning him favor. Many have been drawn towards the gospel he preached, and these formed the nucleus of a Pentecostal church in that part of India.

"Brother Munshie has had many calls to work among small groups of independent Christians scattered here and there throughout eastern Bengal. A hunger for the Pentecostal experience has attended his ministry everywhere, and now he has approximately twenty churches, representing perhaps six hundred people. These are all Christians who look to him for spiritual leadership. He also has about four hundred inquirers in different villages whom he is training for Christian baptism."

There is perhaps no other foreign country where the Pentecostal flame has spread as it has throughout India. Hundreds of missionaries are working to bring the gospel to the hungry millions, and the Lord is adding to the invisible church such as are being saved.

CHAPTER FIFTEEN

Pentecostal Leaders Rebaptized

Frank Small Rebaptized

The following articles or excerpts from articles appeared in various Pentecostal publications in the years 1915 and 1916. Each of the testimonies refers to leading figures in the Pentecostal movement being rebaptized in the name of Jesus.

Printed below is a testimony from Meat in Due Season. *It tells of the rebaptism of Frank Small, who later pioneered a great work in the city of Winnipeg.*

We have received word from Brother Bert Scott that his convention in the Twin Cities has been the best ever held there. Many received the dual baptism, and many who had already received the Holy Ghost got light on the Word concerning water baptism and went down into the watery grave in the precious name of Jesus. Among these was our precious brother in this ministry, Elder Frank Small of Winnipeg, Canada. The truth is spreading at a supernatural rate.

—Meat in Due Season

In a later article published in The Present Truth, *Frank Small gave his personal account of being rebaptized in the name of Jesus. In this article he shares his burden for the city of Winnipeg.*

February 1916. I have been baptized in the name of the Lord Jesus and I have never felt more of His power and presence in my life than since I obeyed His Word (Acts 2:38). This message is growing in my soul and opens up the Scriptures in a new way. I feel sure God is moving His people on, and He is in this great message which is going forth. God has been talking to my heart for some time regarding tent meetings for Winnipeg. The more we pray, the more this fact is impressed upon us. We feel sure the time has come when God is calling upon us to enlarge our borders. A camp meeting will likely develop. Already the way seems to be opening up on these lines. All we want in the matter is the mind of God, and then go ahead. We feel sure that God is coming forth in a revival for Winnipeg. We covet much the prayers of the saints everywhere on our behalf.

—Evangelist F. Small
The Present Truth
Indianapolis, Indiana

Elder R. E. McAlister and Evangelist Harvey McAlister Rebaptized, 1915

The following letter appeared in Living Word *and was written to Brother Scott by Elder G. T. Haywood. Brother Haywood was founder and pastor of Christ Temple in Indianapolis. He was a leader in the Pentecostal movement during his entire ministry. He was well known for his in-depth Bible teaching and was the author of several popular and extremely stirring hymns.*

Dear Brother Scott: Greetings in Jesus. Peace be unto thee and all that are with thee. Peace and love be multiplied through the blood of Jesus Christ our Lord. Amen.

Praise our God for victory through His name. Great is the truth that is going forth in these days. It cannot be hindered. God has given us a sweeping victory here with the message, and the power of God is upon the services.

There have been ninety-two baptized in the name of Jesus in the past two weeks, and more yet to follow. A young woman was converted and filled with the Holy Ghost (New Year's night); as soon as her feet touched the water she began to speak with other tongues—before they could baptize her.

Many have been healed and a number have received the Holy Ghost. We are looking forward to a greater time yet. The unity of the Spirit is very manifest in these services. Brother McAlister and Harvey and their wives were among those baptized. He had wonderfully prepared the people for the message, and when the pool was ready he and his wife were the first to enter the water and the Lord did wonderfully bless us. Yours in Christ, G. T. Haywood.

—*Living Word*
St. Paul, Minnesota

R. E. McAlister Proclaims Belief in Oneness

Below is a letter written by R. E. McAlister in which he affirms his belief in the oneness of God.

Dear Brother Ewart: Greetings in the name of Jesus! Well, we are coming along the line somewhere. I have had a revelation to my soul of the one God in threefold manifestation. How my heart melted in His presence! I could only weep and cry. Greet all the saints for me and tell them I am coming. Love to all the family, in Jesus' name. Yours till He comes, R. E. McAlister, 312 Lisgar Street, Ottawa, Canada, December 15, 1915.

—*Meat in Due Season*

E. N. Bell Baptized in the Name of Jesus

The following report from Evangelist L. V. Roberts appeared in Meat in Due Season *in 1915. It concerns the baptism of E. N. Bell, twice chairman of the Assemblies of God, in the name of Jesus. For some unexplained reason, Brother Bell later recanted his belief in Jesus Name baptism and returned to his advocacy of baptism in the titles Father, Son, and Holy Ghost.*

I have some blessed news to report. God is moving upon the hearts of His people, opening their eyes to the message of today.

I received a telegram last Tuesday from the camp meeting at Jackson, Tennessee, which read: "We want your message for the camp; take first train. Signed, Pastor H. G. Rodgers. E. N. Bell."

It surprised me somewhat at first. Then I remembered that with God all things are possible, and I took the train at once and went over, wishing to know for what intent they had sent for me. I found out very little except they desired to hear the message which we have been declaring is from God. So I opened up with Acts 2:38 as the basis of the message, looking into the message of Peter which opened the way for the declaration of the same, and to my great surprise both E. N. Bell, editor of the *Weekly Evangel* and *Word and Witness*, and the pastor in charge, H. G. Rodgers, accepted the first message and publicly announced before the camp that they were candidates for the water, and the sooner the better.

A voice spoke to Brother Bell before going into this camp that if he did not preach water baptism in the name of Jesus Christ in this camp meeting, things would be a failure, he would dry up, and it would be the worst meeting he had ever conducted; and he found out that things were going that way before sending the telegram for me to come over with the message.

We announced a baptizing for the next afternoon, Brother Bell being the first to be baptized, and had another baptizing, and yet another baptizing on Sunday afternoon. Sixty-eight in all have been baptized in the Name, with more to follow this coming week. Eleven preachers are among the number from all over the South.

The very first meeting after the first baptizing on Friday afternoon was the beginning of a great and mighty outpouring of the Holy Spirit; such blessing and power as had not been before witnessed in the camp. The crowds increased, sinners yielded to God, and a number received the baptism in the Spirit.

The following evening more waves of glory fell, and the meeting continued until after 2:00 o'clock in the morning. A sister commenced to play the piano during the after-service, and the power came upon her and she commenced to play in the Spirit, not knowing what she was playing, and to sing in other tongues to the music, which continued without a break for three hours and forty-five minutes, being timed by Elder J. M. Rowe of 418 Cotton Avenue, Birmingham, Alabama—another mighty sign to the multitude of unbelievers.

On Sunday night we preached the good news to four thousand, according to the estimate of Pastor Rodgers. I left the service and returned home Monday night.

The camp was to have closed on Sunday night, but the meeting had just begun, and meetings were announced to continue indefinitely, both morning and evening.

I expect to make Chicago in a short time, where already Thoro Harris writes me that this message has taken hold upon his heart and desires to see me soon, and said that there was to be a baptizing there next Sunday.

Excerpt from
Meat in Due Season

In this chapter we find an example of the journalistic efforts in the early days of the Pentecostal movement. The following article appeared in Meat in Due Season, *the periodical Ewart edited for several years. Ewart and other Pentecostal leaders used publications to spread the revival and to convince others of the Pentecostal experience.*

The last great crisis is now upon us. The Latter Rain has been falling now for upwards of twelve years in copious showers. The new religion has stirred all Christendom from center to circumference. Lepers have been cleansed; the sick have been healed; the dead have been raised; and the poor have the gospel preached to them in the power of the Spirit. If all the pages were written that might be written about what God has actually wrought since the commencement of this phenomenal revival, it would make a book ten times the size of the Acts of the Apostles.

Christendom has had a chance to accept its distinctive message or turn it down. Most of the nominal churches branded it as of the devil. The rest said emphatically that it was not of God. Men occupying the most eminent positions in the religious world have thrown their influence against it. From platform, pulpit, and press it has been denounced in the most vehement terms. Dr. Campbell-Morgan said, "It was the last vomit of Satan." Dr. Dixon said, "It was wicked and adulterous." Dr. Torrey said, "It was emphatically not of God, and founded by a sodomite." Dr. Pierson said, "It was anti-Christian." Dr. Godbey, in a book called *Tongues and Demons*, denounced it as "sensual and devilish." Indeed if we were to mention all the names of men who are considered great in the realms of Christendom that have bitterly assailed this movement, it would take up all our available space. The difficulty is to find a man with a religious reputation that has not openly declared himself its enemy.

There is no movement since the days of the apostles that has had to fight its way through such unrelenting hatred and bigotry from church and state as this so-called "tongues movement." It has suffered from the hands of its friends as well as its enemies. They have preached its funeral and solemnly laid it to rest with the other religious freaks of history, but like Samuel, it has risen to freeze the blood of its enemies and declare to the Lord's chosen that He has become their enemy, that because they have rejected Him He also has rejected them.

Many a preacher's heart has been touched by this religious outcast's pitiable case. These have invited it to leave off worshiping in old cast-off buildings and vacated storehouses and churches and come in and enjoy the elaborate accommodations of their churches. However, it was not long before such preachers found out that they could no more assimilate this religious nondescript than the whale could assimilate the prophet Jonah. Nearly every member of this movement, especially the ministry, has suffered an experience of expulsion from their churches. However, unlike all other religious movements, it thrives on this kind of treatment.

When the writer of this book received the experience of Acts 2:4, he thought that he could go back and occupy the same pulpit that he left to seek this experience, but he found to his utter surprise that he could no longer adapt himself to his surroundings. This troubled him and he sought the Lord for an explanation. It came and was entirely satisfactory. The Spirit directed him to Isaiah 28:20. On looking up that passage the words stood forth as if they were written in raised type: "The bed is shorter than that a man can stretch himself on it: and the covering narrower than that he can wrap himself in it." This was substantially his position. He was uncomfortable and was relieved when asked to resign.

Since then the Lord has shown me that that this passage describes every creed formed and every system of theology invented since the days of Constantine, when the "faith which was once delivered unto the saints" was lost.[1] It is all deficient and unsuited to the demands of the problem it was formed to solve. We sent missionaries to China and other lands, but they were utterly unable to cope with the appalling situation. However, this gospel is big enough to cope with any situation, and our only limit is because we fail to appropriate Christ in His fullness for our needs. Church missionaries have been baffled by the sight of a single leper, but the faith of the early church was not baffled by any disease known to man. Yea, death itself, was vanquished in the mighty name of Jesus. We believe that the very same power that rocked the world in the apostolic age is available for God's saints today; we only need the faith and daring to claim it. Nothing that God gave to the church has ever been withdrawn in the sense that it cannot be put into operation by faith now.

We have limited the "arm of the Holy One of Israel" by our accursed unbelief. The teaching of the leaders of the nominal churches has backed up doubt instead of faith. They teach that the gifts, including healing and the gift of tongues, were all withdrawn from the church and are unavailable now. Dr. Torrey made the statement "that God withdrew the gift of tongues from the church back in the beginning of the church age, and there was no good reason to say that He had restored it." How utterly absurd! If this were true, then we have a God subject to sudden changes of mind. If He experimented with the gift of tongues and found it a failure, He may have done the same with the other gifts. However, one great passage of Scripture forever settles this matter. What did God say about Himself? "I am the LORD, I change not; therefore ye sons of Jacob are not consumed" (Malachi 3:6).

God's focal purpose in this great latter rain outpouring is to restore the "like precious faith" and power of the apostles and the early church. By one great revolutionary wrench He is lifting His church back over the head of every sect, every creed, every organized system of theology, and putting it back where it was in power, doctrine, and glory on and after the Day of Pentecost. God has been restoring this once-delivered faith in a fragmentary manner. That is the only way we could revive it. It has been "precept upon precept; line upon line, . . . here a little, and there a little" until He brings again Zion, when we shall all see eye to eye. (See Isaiah 28:13.)

Some lepers have been cleansed, but they have not all been cleansed that have been prayed for. Some sick have been healed of incurable diseases, but they have not all been healed. However, it stands recorded in the Acts of the Apostles that the sick were healed every one. On the island of Malta, after the chief was healed, the people brought all their sick and they were healed every one by the laying on of the apostle Paul's hands. What the Pentecostal people have been raised up for in these last days, specifically speaking, is to obey the Word of God just exactly as it stands and believe for apostolic results, and God will confirm His Word exactly as He did back in the beginning. This is what the apostles and saints of the early church did. This is what Jude exhorts us all to do: "Earnestly contend for the faith which was once delivered unto the saints" (Jude 3). The most effective way to contend for it is to demonstrate it by faith. The distinctive faith that Jude spoke of was known as the apostolic faith, and it was a faith based on a definite system of teaching which demonstrated the power to live soberly, righteously, and godly in this present evil world and to heal the sick, cleanse the leper, and raise the dead. The proclamation and the demonstration were inseparable. Great revivals with miraculous signs followed the faithful proclamation of the gospel. The Scripture says that God worked with them and confirmed the Word with signs following (Mark 16:20).

The apostle Paul tells us in Romans chapter 8 "that the whole of God's creation are groaning as in the pangs of childbirth, waiting for the manifestation of the sons of God. And not only they, but we that have received the Spirit, as a foretaste and pledge of the glorious future, yet we ourselves inwardly sigh, as we wait and long for open recognition as sons through the deliverance of our bodies" (Weymouth). It is significant that he does not mention the Rapture or the coming of Jesus or the millennial kingdom. It is the manifestation of the sons of God.

The promise is as true today as it was when Jesus uttered it: "Said I not unto thee, that, if thou wouldest believe, thou shouldest see the glory of God?" (John 11:40). Beloved, the time is at hand! "It remaineth that some must enter therein" (Hebrews 4:6). The manifested sons of God will be those who have walked in God's light and are believing for this very thing. It will be sudden, startling, and revolutionary. It will be a greater surprise in the religious world than the splitting of the atom was in the scientific world. It will have the same revolutionary results as the atomic energy will have in the future life of the world. It will set all hell in pandemonium. It will prove an earthquake shock to the religious world. Priest, prelate, and preacher will turn pale with superstitious awe. Every church pulpit in the earth will rock and fall. Every man's faith will be appraised by the faith once delivered to the saints. It is in proportion to our proximity to that faith how we will fare in Christ's judgment: Some will get sun glory, some moon glory, some star glory, and some inferior star glory. Some will be saved as by fire and some will get a reward. Some will reap multiplied dividends on their investments for the kingdom, but some and perhaps the majority will suffer loss. (See I Corinthians 3:14-15.)

God is going to shake everything that can be shaken, and there is not much time to lose. The fruits of Christ's resurrection will be put on exhibition before this world. Pentecost will be eclipsed in the great end time revival when everyone who calls on the name of Jehovah shall be saved. The name above every name will be revealed in its highest power and glory as it flashes from tongues of fire. Diseases will vanish; death will give way; demons will flee in terror back into the infernal regions from which they came. Hypocrites will be exposed; liars will be struck down; false shepherds will find no cloak for their sins. These will try to drown conviction by persecuting God's people. The courage of martyrdom will again manifest itself. Torches will blaze. The blood will flow, and the cup of the saints' suffering for the name of Jesus will be filled up.

Oh, my brethren! I am thrilled to the depths of my soul. My tongue is like the pen of a ready writer. The sunset of the old life is upon us, and the new order will break in power and great glory. I can say with the inspired poet: "'Tis the sunset of life gives me mystical lore, and coming events cast their shadows before."

The startling characteristics of this great movement are divine healing, speaking with new tongues, and the interpretation of tongues, but those of the new order will be the knowledge of the languages of the nations—as at Pentecost. And prophetic utterance, direct from the indwelling Holy Spirit. The Spirit is speaking expressly. There is not an organization in the entire religious world—Pentecost included—that is ready for this great move of God in the end time. Every comfortable nest will be ruthlessly stirred up. We will have to take the wings of faith. This is the vision! Let us watch for it! For in the end time it will speak and will not lie. The confusion of Babylon will cease, and out of Zion, the perfection of beauty, God will shine. In that day there will be one Jehovah and His name one.

ENDNOTE

[1]Ewart means here that the message of the oneness of God and baptism in the name of Jesus Christ was lost in the church structure adopted by the Roman Empire of which Constantine was emperor. The truth continues to live in the "remnant," the true church.

The Miraculous Resurrection of Joe French

By J. H. Duke

The following testimonial is given to us by J. H. Duke, who resided in Los Angeles at the time of this writing. The miracle described in this chapter is quite representative of the miracles that have taken place on thousands of occasions under the ministry of the twentieth-century Pentecostals. The early apostles experienced such miracles, we are experiencing them today, and we can fully expect them to continue in even greater measure in the future. Whenever the true gospel is preached without reservation, its validity is confirmed by signs and wonders following.

In the month of June 1908, I was in charge of the Railroad Hotel in Thayer, Missouri, on the Frisco Line. One evening about five o'clock while sitting on the veranda, a little Irishman walked up to me and asked me where the manager of the hotel was. I replied that I was the manager. He then asked me if we were in need of a cook. I told him that we were, and he at once presented his claim for the job. He said that he had been chief cook on ocean steamers and had been around the world about five times. I was surprised at this as he had the appearance of a mere boy; however, that is typical of the Irish, as they generally carry their age well. So Joe got the job.

This was just prior to the great revival that broke out in Thayer, and when God began to work, the whole countryside became mightily stirred. The band of saints who came from St. Louis to hold the meetings were entertained at my hotel. These were five in number, namely Mother Barnes; her daughter, Ima Jean; Sister Flint, who conducted a charity hospital in St. Louis; Elder Bennett Lawrence; and Elder H. Bowley, who is a missionary in South Africa. They all enjoyed Joe's cooking and inquired especially as to who made the delicious biscuits. I informed Mother about my little Irish cook and she, being Irish, too, was eager to see Joe.

She found her way to the kitchen, introduced herself to Joe, and at once began to praise his good cooking. Joe was not accustomed to hearing people praise the Lord, and as everyone in that hotel did this, he thought we were a most peculiar crowd. Joe was soon prevailed on to attend the meetings, and one Sunday evening while he was present the speaker referred to the different churches (Catholic included) as being below the apostolic standard. Joe, being a Catholic, instantly got stirred up. The next morning when I went into the kitchen, to my surprise I found Joe breathing out threatenings and slaughter against that preacher for daring to say anything against the Catholic Church.

After some little explanation, the matter was adjusted, and I assured Joe that the preacher loved him and that we all loved him and would do anything in our power to make him happy. The day following, after the train dinner had been served, Joe was suddenly stricken down while in the kitchen. When the two elders entered the kitchen they found Joe in a state of utter collapse and looking as pale as death. They summoned me, and I at once ordered him taken to the main part of the hotel. The two elders had to carry him bodily upstairs to one of the best rooms in the house. Joe asked me to get him the very best doctor we had in the town, so I called Dr. Culp, who after examining the case pronounced it to be malignant typhoid fever, which he said was so fatal that very few ever recovered from it.

Sister Flint, on being told of Joe's condition, felt condemned because she was the only one in the band who had failed to speak to him concerning his soul's salvation. Being a professional nurse, she at once volunteered to nurse him. For eighteen days she faithfully ministered to Joe's wants. On account of her profession she was not strong on divine healing. She administered faithfully all the drugs that the doctor's prescriptions called for, which were numerous. After about five days of Joe's sickness had expired, the marshall of the town came into my office and said, "Mr. Duke, I understand that you have a sick man in this hotel and that you are letting him die for the want of a doctor." I told him that his informant had told a malicious lie, that I had called a doctor at the very outset, and not only that but I had a trained nurse in Joe's room from the commencement also. I insisted that he come up and see for himself. He did so and was dumbfounded when he saw that he had been sent on a fool's errand. This was victory number one.

As time went on Joe became worse. By this time God was working mightily in the meetings. Great crowds looked on from night to night as devils were cast out, the sick healed, and numbers baptized in the Holy Ghost and speaking in other tongues. One morning while in prayer about Joe's condition, I took my Bible and asked God to give me a passage of Scripture regarding his almost hopeless case. It came in a flash. "I am the resurrection, and the life: he that believeth in me, though he were dead, yet shall he live" (John 11:25). I seemed to be able to draw only one meaning from this, as the doctors in a special consultation had pronounced Joe's case utterly hopeless and told me to notify his people to that effect. Try as I would to believe otherwise, there was no alternative but the solid conviction that Joe would surely die but that God would raise him from the dead. The three doctors had emphatically declared that Joe would die before morning, but I informed them that I knew that several days ago, as God had clearly shown me this from His own Word.

That same evening we had one of the most wonderful meetings in the tent I have ever seen. People were lying everywhere slain under the power of God. My wife and I returned to the hotel about 11:00 o'clock and retired for the night. About half past one in the morning I was suddenly awakened by Sister Flint, who was weeping and saying that Joe was dead. I arose and quickly dressed and, on going to Joe's room, found that he was already washed and laid out for burial. I was quite composed in spirit, and walking close by the dead man's side I felt his hands and put my ear close to his heart. There was no sign of life. I turned to Sister Flint and asked her if she were sure that Joe was dead.

"Dead!" she replied, "Have not I seen 150 of them die, and don't I know when a man is dead?"

The Spirit instantly took my tongue and repeated the promise of Scripture that God had given me: "Though he were dead, yet shall he live."

She instantly became so agitated that she derided me, and turning to Mother Barnes, whom I had not noticed, she said, "What do you think of this man?"

Mother Barnes said, "I believe that he believes God." At this the mighty power of God came on me, and before I knew what was happening I was on my knees at the dead man's head, holding him by the hair and rebuking in tongues, the interpretation of which was, "I rebuke this death demon in the name of Jesus and command the spirit to return to this body." Instantly life reentered the body, and Joe's frame shuddered; he opened his eyes and looked straight at Sister Flint.

In a short time Joe became very hungry, and as I had already told Sister Flint to give him anything he asked for, she was ready. When Joe said, "I'm so hungry," she said, "Joey, what can I get for you?" He called for two poached eggs on toast and a glass of milk. This order was quickly brought, which he devoured heartily.

Sister Flint read the Bible to Joe during the remainder of the night and talked to him about his soul, which resulted in his conversion. In the morning while we were all rejoicing over the good news, the doctor stepped in.

He had no medicine case this time, but instead a death certificate. Joe was sitting up in bed with a heavenly smile on his face, and when the doctor saw him he was speechless. We all looked at him and Sister Flint said, "What will we do now, doctor?" He gulped at the lump in his throat and, backing towards the door, muttered, "Keep on praying." He then went out. This was on Friday, and on Sunday Joe was at the meeting seeking the Holy Ghost. The Lord subsequently filled him with the Spirit.

He went back to Ireland and gave himself up to the authorities, confessing a crime of murder and giving the details; but they would not take any note of it, so Joe was clear. He preached the gospel there, and his mother, father, and two sisters were saved and filled with the Spirit. He is now in this country still happy in the Lord. We heard from him recently. It is useless to state that this miracle stirred the town of Thayer and surrounding country and put a living faith in my heart that remains to this day. Why should it be thought incredible with you that God should raise the dead?

Signed, J. H. Duke
145 N. Ditman St.
Los Angeles, California

CHAPTER EIGHTEEN

Early Pentecostal Leaders

At the risk of being judged invidious, we feel incumbent on us to write this chapter and give a number of men whom the Lord has used as key men in the structure of this glorious Latter Rain movement, the honorable mention which they so richly deserve. There are many more who perhaps should be included, but we have to crave the reader's indulgence in the selection we have made. Some of the great men of God have been mentioned elsewhere in these pages, but we felt to include them in this partial list.

The first man of God we would mention is *J. W. Welch*. Because of his fatherly solicitude for others and his kindly bearing, he was familiarly known as Daddy Welch. Brother Welch was gifted with executive ability and served as chairman of the first organization of the apostolic faith movement with great success. One of his characteristics which endeared him to all his many friends was a very rare and original fund of Irish wit. This trait, however, was always limited to the restrictions of reverence and spirituality. It helped to make him the original and rare personality that was known by so many of the saints all over the country and still revered as Daddy Welch.

Howard A. Goss was one of the very earliest ministers to receive the baptism with the Holy Spirit according to Acts 2:4. He received a glorious experience in the great revival that started in Topeka, Kansas, at the beginning of the century. He immediately became prominent in the work of the ministry and was well known for his exceptional piety and devotion to the new cause. When the split in our ranks came on the doctrine of the unity of God, Elder Goss received a revelation of the newly discovered truth and became obedient to the heavenly vision.

He, like all who embraced the new revelation, was greatly opposed by his brethren, but he has maintained his testimony through the years and at this time of writing he is the general superintendent of the United Pentecostal Church, whose distinctive doctrinal tenet is that the Deity is one, not three, and they baptize repentant believers into the name of the Lord Jesus Christ. A great missionary zeal dominates this great organization, and it is growing rapidly both numerically and spiritually. The organizations of the Pentecostal persuasion are making a great impression among the religions of the world. They approximate the apostolic faith more closely than any other religious unit, both in precept and practice. Saints of all the Protestant organizations are contributing to their rapidly increasing membership. Thank God for the great men like our Brother Goss, who are gifted with executive ability and are putting it to use in the work of the Lord.

Glenn A. Cook was one of the very earliest Pentecostal pioneer preachers. He has been identified with the Latter Rain movement from its very inception. After the great revival broke out at Azusa Street Mission in Los Angeles, California, Brother Cook went back into the eastern and southern states of the Union, preaching the distinctive Pentecostal message in the power of the Spirit. Literally thousands were brought into this great experience in his meetings. God gave him the gift of laying on hands for the reception of the Spirit, and so many hundreds received the Holy Spirit under his hands that the enemies of this great work stigmatized him as "Cook the hypnotist." He held successful evangelistic campaigns in Oklahoma, Arkansas, Missouri, and Indiana. Many preachers were brought into this wonderful experience in his meetings, and they in turn were used to spread the Pentecostal revival fires throughout the country.

When the writer received the revelation of the unity of God and the name of Jesus Christ, Brother Cook accepted the message and worked with the writer for many years in and around the city of Los Angeles. Thousands flocked to the new standard in these campaigns. Evangelist Cook is now nearing the eighty-year mark, but he still teaches and preaches wherever opportunity affords.

William H. Durham received his baptism at Azusa Street Mission early in the great revival, and some years later he began to preach a message which was called "The Finished Work of Calvary." It caused a great stir in this movement, as the leaders had unwittingly allowed a doctrine called "sanctification, by a second, definite, instantaneous work of grace" to became a tenet of the faith. Pastor Durham challenged the scriptural stability of this doctrine, and a battle royal resulted. The struggle was fraught with much bitterness, and Pastor Durham soon found himself in the position of a speckled bird among his brethren in this ministry. He stuck to his guns, however, and after a few years the entire movement had swung back and adopted "The Finished Work of Calvary" as orthodox. Sanctification is a progressive work in the development of the Christian graces in the character of the believer. "Having therefore these promises, dearly beloved, let us cleanse ourselves from all filthiness of the flesh and spirit, perfecting holiness in the fear of God" (II Corinthians 7:1). When this view of sanctification was established, the movement was regarded with much more tolerance by the nominal churches, and a great addition from their membership was enjoyed. Durham's campaigns reminded one of the statement of Scripture: "And the word of God increased; and the number of the disciples multiplied . . . greatly; and a great company of priests were obedient to the faith" (Acts 6:7).

Durham passed on to glory at a comparatively early age, but he could say like Paul: "I have fought a good fight, I have finished my course, I have kept the faith" (II Timothy 4:7). He was probably the most original and inspirational preacher of his day, and he influenced this Pentecostal movement for God and righteousness more than any other man. His early death was mourned by all, and thousands will rise up in judgment and call him blessed.

Alfred G. Garr was one of the very earliest, if not the

earliest, of our missionaries to herald the new message in the foreign fields. He was also the first white man to receive the baptism [of the Holy Ghost] at Azusa Street Mission. He and his first wife, who was one of the most profound Bible students and saints that the writer ever met in his long experience, went to India. He was remarkably successful in his ministry among the natives. They attended the Ramabai work, and God used them in a wonderful manner, as Ramabai herself testified. The missionaries already on the field came to conventions that Missionary Garr called, and many of them, seeing the mighty power of God, were obedient to the new faith and received the like precious faith with the apostles. So Brother Garr was used to help the missionary work in India to get on a true, apostolic foundation, and his influence is felt in India missionary fields to this day. Truly "he being dead yet speaketh."

The writer and Elder Garr and his wife worked together for some time and had some wonderful meetings together. Brother Garr was one of the first Pentecostal missionaries to invade China. He was supervisor of the work in Hong Kong for a number of years. In the home fields, A. G. Garr and this writer had some wonderful meetings. However, when the message of the oneness of the Godhead came out, he rejected it, and this caused the very painful parting between us. But despite all these things, our love for each other survived, and this divine love will be renewed in the glory where we will all see eye to eye and doctrinal differences will never again intrude.

George B. Studd, who died in Los Angeles a short time ago at the ripe old age of eighty-five, was the most perfect human I ever met. We worked together for many years in the relationship of pastor and assistant. I had an opportunity of a very intimate association with this wonderful man of God. He was probably beloved by more people than any other man since the days of Dwight L. Moody. He spent a large fortune in the service of the Lord. He did not give his life to the foreign missionary enterprise, but he did give away a large fortune in the propagation of missionary enterprise in the homeland. He had such a great love for the missionaries that every letter that came in from them received his sympathetic consideration. He was one of those rare souls whose life and death was a libation to Almighty God. He was a pillar in the church and a great man in our Israel. Amen!

G. T. Haywood became one of the key men of this great movement. Although a Negro, his influence and power ministered to all races. He was a walking Bible and acknowledged to be one of the outstanding teachers of the Word in his day. He published a paper called *The Voice in the Wilderness*, which was a Pentecostal sledgehammer in its influence in journalism. He also wrote much for other papers and many commendable books. His own people were proud of him and rallied around the high and exalted standard he raised in great numbers.

L. C. Hall was a great adornment to the Latter Rain movement. His influence and power coupled with phenomenal natural ability took him far beyond the range of ordinary ministers. He was pastor, scholar, preacher, poet, songwriter, composer, and one of our best evangelists. With all this striking talent he had one of the most pleasing personalities one could meet and a great heart of love. His tenderness was a part of his genius. I have seen his tears! He will have a high place within the "Temple of the Beautiful."

As the movement swept on in its brilliant course through the vista of time, the early warriors who bore the heat and burden of the hectic day of its early battles and victories gave place to new ones whom God raised up to fill the gaps left in the Pentecostal ranks. One of the most outstanding of these was *William E. Booth-Clibborn.* Born of such spiritually distinctive parentage and raised according to the highest ideals, he had a background that few preachers ever possessed. It was a marvel that he ever came into this Latter Rain movement, but God so ordained it. In his early years he was saved and filled with the Holy Spirit, speaking in other tongues, though none of his own people had this experience at that time. In this country his boyish, burning zeal, buttressed by his sound training and great natural ability, was used of the Holy Spirit to make him one of our most successful evangelists.

W. E. Kidson is now, and has been for two decades, recognized as one of the key men in this movement. His remarkable executive ability was early recognized, and he was elected to a high official position in a Oneness organization, which through the merging of two main bodies of this persuasion later became the United Pentecostal Church. Brother Kidson filled the position of secretary of the Pentecostal Church, Incorporated for a number of office terms until a few years ago. He is now pastor of a growing church in Houston, Texas, and owner of the Herald Publishing House, from whence he publishes a fine Pentecostal paper called *The Herald of Truth*! This paper is enjoying a fine circulation. At a recent revival campaign in Brother Kidson's church, Pentecost was repeated in a remarkable manner, so that through the laying on of Evangelist William Branham's hands, cancers and other incurable diseases were healed, and some blind people had their sight completely restored. When God honors a man's work, the conditions of his heart and life must be eminently scriptural.

Raymond G. Hoekstra of Indianapolis, Indiana, is one of the outstanding figures of this movement. In his church with a seating capacity of approximately one thousand people, there is a constant revival going on. In these meetings the signs and miracles and gifts of the Holy Ghost that characterized the ministry of the apostolic church are not wanting. Recently, a Christian school, recognized by the state, has been erected adjoining the church in which the courses taught in the state schools are taught by competent Christian teachers, and Bible teaching is added to their curriculum. Pastor Hoekstra has a radio broadcast that reaches out to a wide constituency. To know this young man of God is to admire him and love him, and his influence and power under God's blessing is growing by leaps and bounds.

W. T. Witherspoon of Columbus, Ohio, is one of this movement's present outstanding key men. In his large church the presence and power of the Lord of glory is permanently manifested. Elder Witherspoon is also assistant superintendent of the United Pentecostal Church and travels extensively. It is amazing that he can keep going under the hard work and terrific responsibilities involved. Elder Witherspoon is a man with the highest spiritual ideas. He may be classified as a severely righteous man. His spiritual standards in his own church are of the highest scriptural brand, and he is seeking to maintain these same worthy standards in the organization. He believes that Jesus is coming for saints, not theologians or clever preachers or orators, and that the Bible brand of holiness is the highest standard of attainment to which every other qualification should be subordinated. We need more men like this venerable man of God in the pulpits and offices of this great movement.

A. D. Van Hoose is the pastor of a large church in Evansville, Indiana, and has two broadcasts, one in Harrisburg, Illinois, and the other in Del Rio, Texas. He has been used to establish three churches and maintains control of these, being responsible to supply pastors and in other ways to supervise the work. We have watched this young man in his home and in his church and radio work and had the privilege of working with him, and he is the nearest thing to perpetual motion we have ever seen. He has a frail body, but God, the Holy Spirit, vibrates every faculty with His energy. In addition to all his many duties involving such great responsibility, he is the manager and editor of a paper called *The Apostolic Call*. This paper is enjoying a wide circulation and is growing in popularity among Pentecostal saints. His work bulks big among the Apostolic faith churches in the middle states. Although still in the prime of life, Brother Van Hoose has been instrumental in God's hand of getting many preachers converted and baptized in the Holy Spirit. He has sponsored these when they received a call to the work, and rendered them invaluable help in their ministry.

Harry I. Morse has been one of the most efficient of

our ministers in this Latter Rain movement. Brother Morse has enjoyed a long and very successful ministry. He is essentially a pastor and teacher. He has been over thirty years in his present place of abode, and during this time he has been the pastor of a large missionary church. Most of this time he has conducted a training home for missionaries and workers in the homelands. Solid, spiritual, scriptural training has been given the students, and they were put to work in the big downtown mission church in a practical way, and taught how to face an audience, conduct the preliminaries of the meeting, and then they were given training in handling the Word of God.

During these thirty years, Pastor Morse has been famous as a friend and supporter of the missionary cause. He has topped the lists in his state in missionary contributions, and this is a state that has been noted for its missionary liberality. Numbers of our best young workers have received their training and early experiences in Pastor Morse's mission home. A good number of these are successful workers today both at home and abroad.

Brother Morse has always stood for the unity of the Spirit until we all come into the unity of the faith. His policy has been questioned, but on the whole, it has proved eminently successful and practical. I have known Pastor Morse intimately for thirty years, and my every memory of him brings to mind the words of Jesus: "Blessed are the peacemakers: for they shall be called the children of God" (Matthew 5:9). He has passed through long years of hard work and lucrative experiences, which have had the ultimate reaction of developing in him characteristics that are very rich and exceedingly rare. He has a disposition that makes it natural and easy for him to be courteous, gentlemanly, and kind. His influence for God and righteousness throughout the long years and the steady grind has been of the highest quality. I doubt whether any one man has wielded a more beneficent and lasting influence on this Latter Rain movement, and the end is not yet—praise the Lord!

It is hard to stop! But we must, lest our critics will judge us as indulging in much fulsome eulogy. We have tried to give honor to a few out of the many to whom great honor is due. However, in closing this chapter, as we survey the hundreds of great preachers who have crossed our pathway in our rich and long experience in the Latter Rain movement, we feel like saying with the writer of the Epistle to the Hebrews, or rather we feel to paraphrase his immortal words: And what shall we more say? For the time would fail us to tell of Elders Gurley, Ooton, Reeter, Varnell, Brown, Kirby, Stallones, Hite, Lindsay, Cagle, Branding, Lowe, Smith, Wolfe, Tatman, Bisner, Pemberton, David, Rohn, Hurt, Yadon, Baker, Moore, McClain, Johnson, Farrow, White, and Rowe.

These are the men who have built up the structure of this marvelous phenomenon of Pentecost, which in one generation has challenged every unit in the religious world by conforming to the apostolic blueprint in precept and practice, in word and work, and in the absolute identity of accomplishments. Many have hazarded their lives for the name of the Lord Jesus, and some have won a martyr's crown. They form a part of that great company whom the King delighteth to honor, and one day they will be arraigned before the judgment seat of Christ to step out into their respective grades of honor—fair as the moon, bright as the sun, and terrible as an army with banners.

We appreciate the fine spirit of cooperation and the attitude that has been manifested in being willing to assist in any way possible the publication of this, one of the most outstanding books published in these latter days. The following have not only granted permission to use whatever we desired from their own publications, but some have actually assisted in helping to secure additional data: Brothers Stanley H. Frodsham, Frank Small, Glenn A. Cook, Harry Morse, W. F. Carothers, and Pauline E. Parham, daughter of Charles F. Parham.

—W. E. Kidson